The SECRET CODE DATING

Seduction, Dark Psychology, and Manipulation Tactics to Attract and Flirt with Women in the Digital Age. With Video Course and Ready-to-Send Texts

JOE BACHMANN

Copyright © 2024 -Joe Bachmann . All Rights Reserved.

No part of this publication may be reproduced, distributed, or transmitted in any form or by any means, including photocopying, recording, or other electronic or mechanical methods, without the prior written permission of the publisher, except in the case of brief quotations embodied in critical reviews and certain other noncommercial uses permitted by copyright law.

Disclaimer

THE AUTHOR DOES NOT SUPPORT THE USE OF MANIPULATION, NARCISSISTIC ABUSE, OR OTHER DAMAGING TACTICS. INSTEAD THIS BOOK IS A GUIDELINE TO EXPRESSING YOUR PERSONALITY AND ATTRACTING COMPLIMENTARY WOMEN.

TABLE OF CONTENTS

Preface 1

Introduction to the Digital Age of Dating 3

Chapter 1: The Essentials of Attraction 14

Chapter 2: Psychological Hacks for Attraction 33

Chapter 3: Crafting Texts That Get Responses 46

Chapter 4: Expert-Level Texting Tips .58

Chapter 5: Bouncing Back from Rejection and Ghosting 67

Chapter 6: Turning Texts into Real Dates 77

Chapter 7: Video Course Integration .89

Chapter 8: Text Templates That Work .96

Conclusion 103

References 108

PREFACE

Welcome to a journey that might just change your life. If you're picking up this book, chances are you're seeking something more—more confidence, more success, and more fulfillment in your personal relationships. I know exactly how you feel because I've been there.

Not too long ago, I was just like you. Struggling to find my footing in the world of dating, I often felt inadequate and frustrated. I was the guy who watched from the sidelines, envious of those who seemed to naturally attract women and build meaningful connections. My lack of success was a constant reminder of what I believed I couldn't achieve. But everything changed when I decided to take control of my life and embark on a path of self-discovery and growth.

This book is the culmination of that journey. It's about how I went from being an unsuccessful man, uncertain and lacking confidence, to becoming someone who understands social dynamics and has experienced incredible stories with women. My purpose in writing this book is to share my experiences and the lessons I've learned along the way, so you too can transform your life and reach your full potential.

Through countless encounters and many trials, I discovered that success with women—and life in general—is not about luck or inherent charisma. It's about understanding the principles of social interaction, building genuine confidence, and continuously striving to be the best version of yourself. I've experienced the highs and lows, and every step forward was evidence of the fact that change is possible for anyone willing to put in the effort.

Let me be clear: the focus of this book is not to teach you manipulative or weird tactics. This is not about playing games or pretending to be someone you're not. Instead, it's about becoming the best version of yourself and approaching life's opportunities with confidence and authenticity.

It's perfectly natural and fine to work on improving yourself and seizing the chances that come your way.

I remember the frustration, the countless nights wondering why I wasn't good enough, why the guys around me seemed to have it all figured out while I was stuck in the same old rut. I remember thinking, "What the hell am I doing wrong?"

But the truth is, it wasn't about what I was doing wrong; it was about what I wasn't doing right. I wasn't investing in myself. I wasn't taking the necessary steps to grow and evolve. I wasn't pushing my boundaries or challenging myself to become better.

This journey wasn't easy. There were times I wanted to give up, times I thought maybe I was just destined to be that guy forever. But I pushed through. I read, I learned, I practiced, and most importantly, I kept going. Slowly but surely, things started to change. I began to understand the nuances of social interactions, the subtle cues, and the dynamics that can make or break a conversation. I started to build real confidence—not the fake, bravado-filled facade, but genuine, unshakable confidence.

In this book, I'm going to share with you the exact steps I took to turn my life around. You'll learn about the mistakes I made, the lessons I learned, and the strategies I developed. You'll hear about the awkward moments, the embarrassing failures, and the ultimate triumphs.

This isn't just a guide; it's a roadmap based on real experiences. But, you'll find not just advice. There are real stories that illustrate the principles I've come to live by. These stories are meant to inspire and motivate you, to show you that no matter where you're starting from, you can achieve more than you ever thought possible. You might even reach heights you never considered possible, and one day look back and say, "Damn, I fucking made it!"

Whether you're struggling to approach women, build lasting connections, or simply improve your self-esteem, this book will provide you with the tools and insights to turn your life around.

So, buckle up and get ready for an exciting journey. This is about more than just dating; it's about self-development, personal growth, and becoming the man you've always wanted to be.

Remember, every step you take is a step closer to a more confident, successful, and fulfilled version of yourself.

I won't promise it will be easy. There will be challenges, setbacks, and moments where you'll want to throw in the towel. But I can promise you this: if you stick with it—if you commit to the process, you will see results. You will start to feel the changes in yourself, in the way you interact with others, and in the way others perceive you.

Let's begin this journey together and transform our lives, one lesson at a time. You have the power to change your story, to rewrite the narrative of your life. It starts here, and it starts now.

Welcome to your new beginning.
With enthusiasm and conviction,
Joe Bachmann

INTRODUCTION TO THE DIGITAL AGE OF DATING

Dating has gone digital, and if you're not in the game, you're in the dirt. It's a jungle out there, and only the strong survive. It's the new world and your phone's more important than your cologne.

Let me lay it out for you. John, 28, smart enough to code but suffering in the dating world, spends Friday nights swiping without a single match. Then there's Mike, lining up dates like he's booking oil changes. The difference? Mike's cracked the code, and John's still trying to plug in the machine. Here's the truth—Social media's turned dating into a supermarket, and most guys are stuck in the bargain bin. Women are drowning in attention. They're scrolling through an endless buffet of six-pack abs and exotic vacations, thinking the next swipe might land them a billionaire who looks like something from a Hallmark movie.

You're not just competing with the high school jocks anymore. You're up against every guy with a smartphone and the secret to dating. It's a global cock fight, and you need to be the rooster that crows the loudest.

But this new game has got cheat codes, and I'm about to hand them over. The digital age has democratized dating. With the right moves, you can punch way above your weight class. It's not about luck anymore; it's about skill.

Let's break it down:

- ◊ More fish in the sea? Try a whole damn ocean. But more fish means bigger sharks. You need to be at the apex of the food chain.
- ◊ Forget silver tongues. Golden thumbs rule now. If you can't play "game" through a screen, you're dead in the water.
- ◊ Thanks to filters and Photoshop, everyone's presenting perfection but women want realness (that's one of those secrets).
- ◊ It's speed dating on crack. What used to take months now happens in minutes. You have to know how to garnish attention and maintain it.
- ◊ Google: your new wingman. Everyone's researchable. Use it to your advantage before she uses it against you.
- ◊ Ghosting, breadcrumbing, orbiting. Learn the lingo or get lost in translation.

This isn't about cheap tricks or fake personas. It's about becoming the ultimate version of yourself and showcasing it in the digital arena. It's about understanding what makes women tick in the age of Instagram and using that knowledge to create real attraction. The digital dating age is here. You can either adapt and conquer or get swiped left into oblivion.

▌ *Your choice!*

The Challenges Men Face in Modern Dating

Modern dating isn't just a game; it's a gauntlet—and if you're not prepared, it'll chew you up and spit you out.

Let's dive into the goat rodeo that is modern dating for men.

First up, social anxiety and fear of rejection. Let's be real, most of us are walking around with less confidence than a deer in the middle of the jungle.t. You're so afraid of rejection, that you'd rather swipe endlessly than risk talking to a real, live woman. Science time, guys. There's this thing called rejection sensitivity. It's your brain being an overprotective buzzkill, trying to shield you from social pain (Downey & Feldman. 1996). See, back in the caveman days, rejection could mean death. No tribe, no food, no survival. Your brain's still stuck in that prehistoric bullshit, making you feel like a woman saying "no" is equivalent to a saber-tooth tiger eyeing you for dinner. The truth is that rejection won't kill you. It might sting your ego, but last I checked, no one's died from a bruised ego. The real death lies in not trying. Every shot you don't take is a guaranteed miss. You're not preserving your dignity by avoiding rejection; you're just cockblocking yourself.

Now, let's talk about the paradox of choice. You'd think having thousands of potential matches at your fingertips would be a dream come true. Wrong. It's a fustercluck nightmare. You're drowning in options, paralyzed by the fear that the next swipe might be "the one." Let's get this straight. There is no "the one." There's only the one you choose and make it work with. This paradox of choice is messing with your head. You're so afraid of making the wrong choice that you end up making no choice at all. You're like a dog chasing cars—you wouldn't know what to do if you caught one. Stop treating women like menu items you have no intention of ordering.

And let's not forget about decision fatigue. It's a real thing, backed by science. Your brain has a limited amount of mental energy for decision-making. The more choices you make, the worse your decisions become. Here's the science because being alpha isn't about having the facts locked and loaded: Dr. Roy Baumeister, a psychologist, found that our willpower and decision-making abilities decline throughout the day as we make more choices (Vohs et al. 2008). It's like a muscle that gets tired. So when you're endlessly swiping and chatting, you're burning through your mental energy. By the time you've swiped through a hundred profiles, you're about as sharp as a marble.

The modern dating landscape is a minefield of other challenges:

- ◊ **The Instagram effect:** Everyone's projecting their highlight reel. It's like trying to have a relationship with a billboard.
- ◊ **The attention economy:** Women are drowning in male attention online. Your message is competing with hundreds of others. Standing out isn't just important; it's fricking crucial.
- ◊ **The death of courtship:** Old school courtship is dead. Now it's all about sliding into DMs and hoping your emoji game is strong enough.
- ◊ **The ghosting epidemic:** People disappear faster than donuts at a police station. You could be having a great conversation one minute, and the next? Radio silence. It's enough to give a man trust issues.
- ◊ **The expectation of instant chemistry:** Thanks to rom-coms and dating shows, everyone's expecting fireworks from the first message. To all the impatient types: real connections take time.
- ◊ **The pressure to be perfect:** With so many options available, any minor flaw can be a deal-breaker. You need to be funny, smart, successful, fit, and emotionally available. Oh, and throw in a dog. Everyone loves dogs.
- ◊ **The tech gap:** Not everyone's tech-savvy. If you can't navigate multiple dating apps while keeping up witty banter on Instagram and scheduling a date on WhatsApp, you're already behind.
- ◊ **The race against time:** Everything moves at lightning speed. You snooze, you lose. That match you've been meaning to message? She's already gone on three dates since you matched.
- ◊ **The validation vortex:** Dating apps can become addictive. The rush of getting a match, the thrill of a new message—it's like a slot machine in your pocket. You start caring more about the validation than actual connections.
- ◊ **The reality check:** Meeting in person after weeks of texting can be a shock. That witty, charming persona you've been talking to might turn out to be a dud in real life. It's like ordering a steak and getting served overcooked liver.

Now, I know what you're thinking. "How am I supposed to navigate all this?" Well, that's exactly what I'm here to teach you.

First step: Grow a pair. Seriously. Half of these challenges exist because you let them. Social anxiety? Push through it. Fear of rejection? Embrace it. Paradox of choice? Make a damn choice and stick with it. Here's your new mantra: "Screw it, I'll do it live." Stop overthinking every interaction. Stop treating every match like it's your last. Stop putting women on pedestals. They're people, just like you, with their own insecurities and challenges.

Remember, in the land of the blind, the one-eyed man is king. Most guys are stumbling around in the dark, making the same mistakes over and over. By simply being aware of these challenges, you're already ahead of the game. But awareness isn't enough. You need action. You need to start putting yourself out there, making mistakes, learning from them, and growing.

Every rejection, every ghosting, every bad date is a lesson. It's all data you can use to improve your approach.

The Importance of Confidence and Communication

Confidence and communication aren't just buzzwords; they're your lifeline in this chaotic dating world. So let's break this down and build you up.

Tackling the Challenges

◊ **Social Anxiety and Fear of Rejection**

You're not a lightweight, so stop acting like one. Fear isn't your master; you are.

- **Action:** Today, look a stranger in the eye and say something—anything. Move from small talk to meaningful conversations, and before the day is over, approach a woman you find attractive. You will not leave the situation without making your intentions clear.

Gradually work your way up to approaching women. Remember, rejection won't kill you, but your fear of it will block you for life. So, make a plan to take these small actions today and keep pushing your boundaries.

◊ **Paradox of Choice and Decision Fatigue**

Stop treating Tinder like it's an all-you-can-eat buffet.

- **Action:** Right now, set your standards, and if someone doesn't meet them, swipe left without a second thought. When you match, set up a date within the first three exchanges. No more mindless chatting. Decide and act—today.

Your time is precious—act like it.

◊ **The Instagram Effect**

Cut the bull. Your profile should be you, not some fake version you think women want.

- **Action:** Today, strip away the filters, the fake smiles, and the poses. Show who you really are and what you genuinely care about. Post something that reflects your real interests and values, not what you think others want to see.

It's a lot easier to maintain a real persona than a fake one. Authenticity attracts.

◊ **The Attention Economy**

Stand out by being genuinely interesting, not by being a try-hard douchebag.

- **Action:** Be the man who has something to say. Today, share an opinion, start a new hobby, or dive deeper into an existing passion. Do something that adds depth to who you are, and make it a point to talk about it the next time you meet someone new.

You're not just another profile; you're a person with substance—prove it.

◊ **The Death of Courtship**

Bring that fire back to life. Be bold.

- **Action:** Today, ask someone out in person—no excuses. Make the effort, plan the date, and show her that you're not just another guy who hides behind screens.

Stand out by being the one who brings real connection back into dating. No more lazy texting

◊ **The Ghosting Epidemic**

Grow a thick skin—if someone ghosts you, their loss.

- **Action:** You're better than that. If you're not interested, say so clearly and respectfully—today. Set the standard for how you expect to be treated by treating others with respect.

You're here to win, not to wallow.

◊ **The Expectation of Instant Chemistry**

Manage expectations—yours and hers. Rome wasn't built in a day, and neither are meaningful connections.

- **Action:** Real connections take time. Today, commit to giving your dates more than one chance before making a judgment.

Patience is your new strategy. Invest in it, and it will pay off in ways you can't imagine. Be willing to walk away if it's not working. Don't force something that isn't there. You're not at a charity auction.

◊ **The Pressure to Be Perfect**

You're not perfect, and neither is she.

- **Action:** Stop chasing perfection. Right now, embrace your imperfections and be unapologetically yourself.

Flaws make you human. Perfect is overrated. Interesting is alpha. Show her your scars, metaphorically speaking. They tell your story.

◊ **The Tech Gap**

Get comfortable with technology, but don't let it rule you.

- **Action:** Today, take every conversation offline as soon as possible. Set up a meeting, get face-to-face, and make it happen.

Use tech as a tool, not a crutch. Remember, the goal is to meet in person, not to become pen pals.

◊ **The Race Against Time**

Slow the heck down.

- **Action:** You set the pace. Today, put down your phone for an hour and focus on something that matters—whether it's a hobby, a workout, or planning your next date.

Quality connections aren't built on speed dial. Be responsive, but don't be a slave to your phone. Desperation is for drowning men grabbing at straws.

Confidence

> *Confidence is the key to the whole freaking kingdom. It's the backbone of a man's magnetism. It's the power tie of masculinity. Period. It's more important than your looks, your job, or the size of your bank account. Why? Because confidence signals to a woman's primitive brain that you're a capable provider and protector. It's evolutionary psychology, boys.*

True confidence isn't about being an arrogant ass. It's about being comfortable in your own skin. It's about knowing your worth and not seeking validation from others. It's about being able to walk into a room and own it, not because you think you're better than everyone else, but because you're secure in who you are. It draws people to you like moths to a flame. When you're confident, you naturally become more charismatic. You speak with authority. You carry yourself with purpose. Women pick up on this instinctively. It's like catnip for their attraction centers. But confidence isn't just about attracting women. It's about how you handle rejection, how you deal with challenges, and how you navigate the ups and downs of dating. A confident man doesn't crumble when a girl says no. He doesn't lose his head when he gets ghosted. He knows his value doesn't depend on any one person's opinion of him.

And, you don't fake confidence. You build it:

- Set a goal that scares you, and crush it—today. No hesitation, no second-guessing. Make it happen.
- Hit the gym—today. No excuses. Build a body that reflects your inner strength.
- Master a new skill—immediately. Confidence comes from competence.
- Confront your biggest fear—this week. Look it in the eye and take it down.
- Stop negative self-talk—now. Speak to yourself like a champion, because that's what you are.
- Elevate your style—today. Dress like the man you aspire to be.
- Fix your posture—this instant. Stand tall, shoulders back, and walk with purpose.
- Say "no" more often—starting today. Your boundaries are non-negotiable.
- Celebrate every win, no matter how small—today. Confidence is built brick by brick.
- Turn every failure into a lesson—right now. There's no such thing as a loss, only feedback.

There's no shortcut, no magic pill. You want confidence? Learn it then earn it. Get out there and earn it—today, not tomorrow, not next week. Now.

Communication

Now, let's talk about communication. In the world of dating, your words are your weapons. Use them wisely.

- **First principle:** Listen more than you talk. Most guys are so busy trying to impress a woman that they forget to pay attention to her. Active listening is a power. It shows you're interested, it helps you understand her better, and it gives you material to work with in the conversation. Don't just wait for your turn to speak. Actually, hear what she's saying.
- **Second principle:** Ask good questions. Not boring milksop like "What do you do?" or "Where are you from?" Ask about her passions, her dreams, and her opinions. Make her think. Make her feel interesting. "What's the craziest thing you've ever done?" "If you could change one thing about the world, what would it be?" These questions lead to real conversations.

- **Third principle:** Be honest. Don't try to be someone you're not. If you don't know something, admit it. If you're nervous, own it. Honesty is refreshing in a world of bullshitters. Plus, it's a lot easier to remember the truth.

- **Fourth principle:** Use humor. Women love a man who can make them laugh. But remember, there's a fine line between funny and try-hard. Self-deprecating humor can work but don't overdo it. You want her to laugh with you, not at you. And for the love of all that's healthy, no crude jokes on the first date.

- **Fifth principle:** Be direct. Say what you mean and mean what you say. No games, no manipulation. If you're interested, say so. If you want to see her again, ask her out. Directness is attractive because it shows confidence. It also saves both of you time and energy.

- **Sixth principle:** Learn to read between the lines. Communication isn't just about words. Pay attention to body language, tone of voice, and what's not being said. Is she leaning in? Good sign. Arms crossed? Maybe not so good. Learn to pick up on these cues.

- **Seventh principle:** Know when to shut up. Sometimes, silence is powerful. Learn to be comfortable with pauses in conversation. Don't feel the need to fill every moment with words. Let the tension build.

- **Eighth principle:** Be positive. This doesn't mean you have to be fake cheerful all the time, but generally, keep the vibe upbeat. Save your existential crisis for your therapist, not your date.

- **Ninth principle**: Use her name. It's personal, it shows you're paying attention, and it creates a connection. Don't overdo it, but sprinkle it in throughout the conversation.

- **Tenth principle:** End conversations on a high note. Leave her wanting more, not checking her watch. Always be the one to end the interaction first. It keeps you in control and leaves her intrigued.

But you can't just mimic these behaviors and expect results. This isn't about putting on an act. It's about becoming the kind of man who naturally embodies these qualities. Start incorporating these principles into your conversations every day: listen actively, ask one meaningful question, and use her name to build rapport. And that's the real challenge. It's not about learning a few tricks or pickup lines. It's about personal growth. It's about becoming the best version of yourself. It's about developing real confidence, not just in dating, but in all areas of your life.

This stuff takes work. It takes commitment. It takes balls. But the payoff? It's worth it. Because when you develop true confidence and master the art of communication, you don't just become better at dating. You become better at life.

Are you ready to put in the work? Are you ready to stop whining about how hard dating is and start dominating the game? Are you ready to turn these challenges into your personal playground? Ready to become the guy that makes phones light up like Christmas trees?

Remember, in the jungle of modern dating, you're either the predator or the prey. And I didn't just spend all this time turning you into a lion for you to act like a freaking gazelle. So here's your opportunity: Be the guy who gets it.

Freebie Alert: Grab Your Textual Viagra Here!

You're probably wondering where the bloody hell you're supposed to dig up this template gold. Come on, I won't leave you high and dry. I'm the bearer of gifts and that's why I present to you the epic lead magnet: Text SO Good She Can't Ignore You and the Adiobook Bonus!Just scan the QR code and watch the floodgates of prose swing wide open, you lucky man. Inside you'll find templates, smoother than a fresh jar of Skippy, conversation starters that'll have her replying faster than you can say "dick pic" (don't you freaking dare).

But here's the kicker—this shit's free. That's right, free. No strings attached!

So what are you waiting for, an engraved invitation? Whip out that phone and scan that QR code!

CHAPTER 1: THE ESSENTIALS OF ATTRACTION

> *There's Mike—average looks, average job, nothing special. But when Mike walks into a bar, it's like Moses parting the Red Sea—women swoon.*
>
> *Mike's got something—he understands the essentials of attraction.*

Last Friday, I watched this magnificent creature in action. He strolls in, confidence oozing from every pore. No peacocking, no cheesy pickup lines. Just raw, unapologetic Mike. He spots a woman at the bar. Most guys would've chickened out entirely or tried some lame-ass approach. Not Mike. He walks up and says, "I bet you're tired of guys buying you drinks. How about you buy me one instead?"

Ballsy move? Hell yes! But it worked. Why? Because it flipped the script. It showed confidence. It made him stand out from the thirsty simps she's used to. Two hours later, Mike's leaving with her number and a date lined up. Meanwhile, a dozen other guys are drowning their sorrows, wondering why they struck out.

Mike's not special. He's not rich. He's not a model. But here's the kicker—Mike takes care of himself. He's got a solid build, dresses sharp, and always looks like he's ready to take on the world. Why? Because Mike knows that physical appearance is more than just looks—it's a sign of self-love. When you respect yourself enough to stay in shape, dress well, and carry yourself with pride, people notice. They see that you value yourself, and that's magnetic.

And that is what you're about to learn.

Psychological Principles of Attraction

What triggers attraction? This isn't some cosmic bullshit or your grandma's dating advice. This is hardcore science, the kind of knowledge that separates the alpha males from the sniveling beta bunglers.

Let's start with the science behind attraction.

The Science Behind Attraction

Similarity

Similarity. You heard that right. Turns out, people aren't looking for their opposite. They want someone who's on their wavelength. Here's the breakdown:

- ◊ **Shared interests:** If you both get a hard-on for vintage vinyl or lose your shit over the same sports team, you're already halfway in.
- ◊ **Common values:** Do you both think cheating is for reprobates? Congratulations, you've got a foundation that isn't made of bullshit.
- ◊ **Similar backgrounds:** Grew up in the same kind of neighborhood? Instant connection. It's like you're both members of a secret club, only the secret is your shared childhood experiences.
- ◊ **Similar education levels:** People tend to marry those with similar educational backgrounds. This similarity can reflect shared intellectual interests and life goals.
- ◊ **Similar levels of attractiveness**: The "matching hypothesis" suggests that people tend to pair up with others of similar physical attractiveness.

The similarity-attraction effect was first proposed by Byrne and has been consistently supported by research (Byrne. 1961). A meta-analysis by Montoya confirmed that similarity is indeed a strong predictor of attraction in both existing and potential relationships (Montoya & Horton. 2012).

Why does this similarity shit matter? Because familiarity breeds comfort. When we're with someone similar, our brains don't have to work as hard to understand and predict their behavior. This reduces stress and increases attraction. You're not constantly on edge, wondering if they're going to judge you.

But don't get too comfortable, because here comes the shallow part: physical attractiveness.

Physical Attractiveness

You thought your stellar personality would be enough? Tough shit. Let's call a spade a spade. Here's the deal:

- ◊ **Symmetrical facial features:** If your face looks like it was put together by a toddler playing with Mr. Potato Head, you're gonna have a hard time.
- ◊ **Clear skin:** Acne isn't exactly a game-changer. It never has been, it never will be.
- ◊ **Healthy appearance:** Looking like you might keel over at any second is not a turn-on. Hit the gym—and eat a steak once in a while.

Why do these physical traits matter? It's all about good genes and reproductive health. On a primal level, we're all just trying to make babies that won't be a complete evolutionary dead-end. Your clear skin and symmetrical face are billboards saying, "My genes are top-notch, let's make some top-notch kids!" It's human.

Here's the kicker: while physical attractiveness is important for initial attraction, its importance decreases over time in long-term relationships. Moreover, what's considered physically attractive can vary across cultures and change over time. While some features (like clear skin and facial symmetry) are universally attractive, others are culturally specific (Little et al. 2011). It's also worth noting that people tend to become more physically attractive to us as we get to know and like them. This is known as the "propinquity effect" (Propinquity Effect. n.d.). And, to take things up a notch; your physical appearance is a sign of self-love. Taking care of yourself—through grooming, fitness, and style—reflects self-respect and confidence. It's not about being a chiseled Adonis; it's about showing you value yourself enough to put in the effort. Just look at men before and after a decent beard trim and haircut; the transformation is real. So, don't sweat it if you're not a cover model. It's not a dead end. Personality and self-care are your tickets to enhancing your appeal and showing the world you're worth the look.

But don't implode if you're not God's gift to eyeballs. It's not a dead end because personality traits matter too—and there are ways to work on that symmetry (seriously, check out pictures of men before and after proper beard grooming and a haircut).

Personality Traits

Women find certain qualities attractive, and lucky for you, these can be developed. Here's what the ladies are looking for:

> **Confidence:** *This is the holy grail of attractive traits. Not to be confused with being an arrogant prick. Real confidence is knowing your worth without having to shove it down everyone's throat. It's about carrying yourself with self-assurance. Here's what real confidence looks like:*

- ◊ You know your worth, but you don't need to constantly prove it.
- ◊ You can take rejection without crumbling like a sandcastle.
- ◊ You're not afraid to voice your opinions, even if they're unpopular.
- ◊ You can admit when you're wrong without having an existential crisis.

Developing confidence isn't about faking it till you make it. It's about building a solid foundation of self-worth.

> **Humor:** *If you can make her laugh, you're golden. But we're talking actual humor here, it needs to be genuine. Women can smell try-hard humor from a mile away. Here's how to actually be funny:*

- ◊ Develop your observational skills. The best humor comes from pointing out the absurdities of everyday life.
- ◊ Learn to laugh at yourself. Self-deprecating humor shows you don't take yourself too seriously.
- ◊ Timing is everything. A well-timed quip is worth a thousand forced jokes.
- ◊ Know your audience. What's hilarious to your bros might not fly on a date.

The goal is to make her laugh with you, not at you. If your humor is always at someone else's expense, you're not funny, you're just an asshole.

> **Kindness**: *It turns out that being a decent human being is attractive. Who knew? This might seem at odds with the alpha male image you're trying to project, but kindness is strength, not weakness. Here's the truth: kindness shouldn't be a transactional game where you're expecting sexual rewards as your return on investment. Many guys screw this up, thinking that being nice is just a clever ploy to get laid or that their sweet gestures should automatically lead to a hookup. Newsflash: that's not true kindness; that's a manipulative script.*

Real kindness comes from a genuine place. It's about treating people well without keeping score or expecting anything in return. You want to be a true badass? Be kind because it's the right thing to do, not because you think it's going to score you points. That's what makes you stand out—not the calculated moves, but the authentic, no-strings-attached decency.

So, forget about using kindness as a bargaining chip and focus on being genuinely good-hearted. That's where true attraction lies.

Here's what it looks like:

◊ You treat service staff with respect. Nothing dries up a woman faster than seeing you be an ass to the waiter.

◊ You show empathy. Being able to understand and share the feelings of others is hotter than a microwaved burrito at midnight.

◊ You're considerate. Small gestures that show you're thinking of others go a long way.

◊ You stand up for what's right, even when it's not convenient.

Kindness doesn't mean being a pushover. It's about having the strength to be gentle. It means being secure enough in yourself to treat others with respect and compassion. *Kindness Disclaimer—Don't be kind and expect sex for it!*

Intelligence: *We're talking about genuine curiosity and the ability to engage in conversations that don't revolve around beer and sports. Here's how to flex:*

◊ Stay informed about the world. Read the news, form opinions, and be able to discuss current events without sounding like a conspiracy theorist.

◊ Develop interests beyond the superficial. Have hobbies that challenge you mentally.

◊ Ask questions and actually listen (active listening) to the answers. Show genuine interest in learning new things.

◊ Be able to explain complex ideas in simple terms. True intelligence is being able to make difficult concepts understandable.

Intelligence is attractive because it suggests you can hold your own in a variety of situations. It shows you're adaptable and capable.

These traits don't exist in isolation. They work together to create an overall attractive package. A confident man who can make a woman laugh, treat others with kindness, and engage in stimulating conversation? That's a rare breed in the dating jungle.

But here's the secret that most guys miss: These traits aren't just about attracting women. *They're about becoming a better man.* When you develop these qualities, you're not just improving your dating life. You're improving your whole damn life.

You'll be more successful at work. You'll have better relationships with friends and family. You'll be more resilient in the face of life's challenges. In short, you'll be the kind of man that others look up to and want to be around. Think Tony Stark. Stop focusing on cheesy pickup lines and start focusing on personal growth. Develop your confidence, hone your humor, cultivate kindness, and sharpen your mind. Attraction is about becoming the best version of yourself. It's about being such a magnificent man that women can't help but be drawn to you.

The world needs men of substance, men of character!

Building Self-Confidence

Time to tackle the cornerstone of attraction: self-confidence. This isn't puffing out your chest or swanning around like you've got the crown jewels. Real confidence comes from within, it's unshakeable.

Techniques for Boosting Self-Esteem

Forget the feel-good crap; this is the real deal, the nitty-gritty of becoming a man who owns his shit.

Positive Self-Talk

You've got talents and achievements, so start acknowledging them. Focus on your strengths and accomplishments. Get out there and brag about your victories—loudly and proudly. Did you crush that presentation at work? That's worth celebrating. Can you bench press your body weight? Hell, that's impressive. Stop downplaying your wins and start owning them.

But listen up, because this is where the rubber meets the road. It's your life—your journey, your story—and every single day, you've got the choice to do or not do things that advance you in life. Read that again. You're at the wheel, and the direction you take is entirely up to you. Each morning when you wake up, you're staring down two paths: one that pushes you forward, challenges you, and makes you stronger, and another that keeps you stuck in the same old rut, spinning your wheels in the mud of complacency. Here's the kicker: nobody's going to make that choice for you. No one's going to drag you out of bed and onto the path of progress. You have the power to level up or stay in the same place. And let's be real—staying in the same place isn't just about comfort; it's a slow descent into stagnation. The world keeps moving, and if you're not moving with it, you're falling behind.

So take a hard look in the mirror and ask yourself: are you going to be the guy who lets opportunities pass by, stuck in the endless loop of "what ifs" and "I wish I hads"? Or are you going to be the guy who grabs life by the horns, makes bold moves, and refuses to settle for anything less than progress? This isn't just a pep talk—it's a wake-up call. You've got the power, the choice, and the control. The only question is, what are you going to do with it? The road to leveling up isn't paved with luck or chance; it's built with decisions, with every small step that leads you closer to where you want to be. So don't just read these words—live them. Make the choice today, tomorrow, and every day after that to push yourself forward. Because if you don't, you're not just staying the same—you're falling behind.

Remind yourself daily of your positive qualities. Are you loyal? Hardworking? Creative? These aren't just nice-to-haves; they're the building blocks of your character. And when that little inner heckler in your head starts whining about your flaws? Tell it to shut its cake hole. You messed up a date? Big deal. Instead of crying about it, learn from it. You're not an idiot; you're a guy who's leveling up.

> *Your mind believes what you tell it! So, tell yourself you're unstoppable and mean it.*

Practice and Preparation

Confidence isn't about winging it; it's about being ready for anything. Prepare like a pro.

Have some killer conversation starters locked and loaded. "What's the craziest thing you've done this year?" beats the hell out of "So, uh, what do you do?" And for the love of all that's holy, plan your dates. Don't be that dipshit frantically Googling "fun first date ideas" while she's on her way. Don't be caught off guard; have a list of regular spots and activities you would both enjoy on hand. Be the man with a plan. Practice how you'll handle common dating situations. How will you gracefully end a date that's not going well? What will you say if she asks about your ex?

Preparation is your secret weapon. Being prepared eases anxiety and allows your natural charm to shine through. It's not about being rigid; it's about having a solid foundation to improvise from.

Setting Achievable Goals

This is where the rubber meets the road. You need to be an ambitious overachiever. Let's talk about SMART goals.

SMART stands for Specific, Measurable, Achievable, Relevant, and Time-bound. It's a framework for not screwing up your goal-setting:

- ◊ **Specific:** Make them specific. "Get in shape" is about as useful as a screen door on a submarine. "Hit the gym three times a week, for an hour per day, for a month"—now that's something you can sink your teeth into.
- ◊ **Measurable:** If you can't measure it, you can't manage it. Numbers are your friends here, gents.
- ◊ **Achievable:** Don't set yourself up for failure. Challenge yourself, but keep it in the realm of possibility.
- ◊ **Relevant:** Make sure your goal aligns with your bigger picture. Don't waste time on bullshit that doesn't matter.
- ◊ **Time-bound:** Set a deadline. "Someday" is not a day of the week.

Now, let's add some rocket fuel to your goal-setting:

Break it down: *Big goals are intimidating. Chop them into smaller, manageable pieces. Want to land a hottie? Start with "Strike up conversations with three new women this week."*

Visualize success: *See yourself crushing your goals. Feel it. Smell it. Taste it. Your brain can't tell the difference between vivid imagination and reality.*

Write that shit down: *Put your goals on paper. It makes them real and holds your ass accountable.*

Create a ritual: *Link your goals to daily habits. Want to be more confident? Start each day with a power pose and positive affirmations. Yes, it feels stupid at first. Do it anyway.*

Track your progress: *Use an app, a journal, whatever. Just keep score. Seeing progress is like crack for motivation.*

Reward yourself: *Hit a milestone? Treat yourself. But make the reward match the achievement. Don't buy a bloody Rolex for remembering to brush your damn teeth.*

Surround Yourself with Positive People

Your environment shapes you, so make sure it's molding you into the best version of yourself. Surround yourself with winners, not whiners.

Begin by upgrading your human ecosystem and hang with people who push you to be better. Audit your friendships. Who's dragging you down? Who's lifting you up? Make a list and be brutally honest. Cut the dead weight. It's not personal, it's an improvement.

Once you've completed your audit, seek mentors. Find someone who's where you want to be. Buy them coffee. Pick their brain. Emulate their success. Mentors and high-value friendships can also be found in hanging with high-value groups. Find clubs, classes, or meetups aligned with your goals. Fitness groups, entrepreneurship circles, whatever.

If you can't find your tribe locally? Go online. Join forums, Facebook groups, or subreddits aligned with your interests. While we're talking about being online—upgrade your media diet. The content you consume shapes your mind. Follow motivational accounts, read success stories, and listen to podcasts that challenge you.

Finally, you need to create accountability partnerships. Find a buddy with similar goals, check in regularly, and push each other. This ensures you're not fueling a dead fire with the both of you becoming deadbeat losers who do nothing to achieve anything. Make sure these accountability partners are savvy and have the same values as you. You never want to be the smartest person in the room, because if you are, you're in the wrong bloody room. Surround yourself with ambition but also be of value and bring something to the table. Be the person others want to be around. Look, you can't always cut people out entirely but you can learn to tune out negativity when you have to be around it.

Remember, you're the average of the five people you spend the most time with. So choose wisely, or you'll end up as mediocre as a gas station sandwich.

Additional Techniques for Boosting Confidence

> **Own Your Space**: *Command the room with your presence. Whether it's your workspace, your living area, or a social setting, make it clear you're not just occupying space—you're owning it. Personalize your environment so it reflects your personality and strengths. This makes you feel more grounded and confident.*
>
> **Develop a Growth Mindset**: *Embrace challenges as opportunities for growth rather than obstacles. Adopt a mindset that values learning over instant success.*

Instead of stressing over mistakes, view them as part of your journey to greatness. Remember, the only way out is through.

Craft a Personal Mission Statement: *Define your core values and goals with a personal mission statement. This isn't just corporate mumbo jumbo; it's your personal north star. Knowing what you stand for and where you're heading keeps you grounded and focused, boosting your confidence as you align your actions with your values.*

Host and Participate in Social Events: *Take charge by organizing social events or gatherings. Being the host gives you a sense of authority and control. Plus, it's a great way to practice social skills and build networks. Don't wait for invitations—create your own opportunities.*

Learn to Master the Art of Conversation: *Sharpen your conversational skills by practicing active listening and engaging dialogue. Ask open-ended questions and show genuine interest in others. Good conversation isn't just about talking; it's about connecting. The more adept you become, the more confident you'll feel in social situations.*

Create a Confidence Ritual: *Develop a pre-confidence-boosting ritual. It could be something as simple as a quick workout, a motivational playlist, or a power pose. This ritual primes your mind and body for confidence and helps you shake off nerves before important events or meetings.*

Practice Assertiveness: *Learn to express your needs, desires, and boundaries clearly and confidently. Being assertive doesn't mean being aggressive; it's about standing up for yourself while respecting others. Role-play different scenarios to practice assertive communication until it feels natural.*

Explore New Experiences: *Step out of your routine and try something new—travel to a new place, pick up a new hobby or take a class in something totally unrelated to your usual interests. Novel experiences build resilience and broaden your perspective, enhancing your self-assurance.*

Visualize Success with Detail: *Instead of vague visualizations, create detailed mental images of your success. Picture every step of achieving your goals, from overcoming challenges to celebrating victories. The clearer your vision, the more real and attainable your success will feel.*

Join Public Speaking or Toastmasters: *Challenge yourself with public speaking engagements or join a Toastmasters club. Mastering the art of public speaking is one of the most potent confidence boosters. Plus, it's a fantastic way to develop poise and articulation.*

Develop a Personal Brand: *Define and cultivate a personal brand that reflects your strengths and values. Whether it's through social media, professional networking, or personal interactions, a strong personal brand helps you project confidence and credibility.*

Seek Professional Development: *Invest in courses, workshops, or certifications that enhance your skills and knowledge. Continuous learning not only improves your capabilities but also reinforces your confidence in your expertise and value.*

Implementing these strategies isn't a walk in the park. It's more like a sprint through a minefield. It's gonna be uncomfortable. You'll doubt yourself. You'll want to quit. But that's where the magic happens, in that space between your comfort zone and total flaming chaos. So, are you ready to set goals that actually mean something and surround yourself with people who aren't human participation trophies?

Now, let's tackle one of the biggest obstacles to confidence: Negative self-talk.

Overcoming Negative Self-Talk

It's time to wage war on that nagging voice in your head that's been holding you back. You know the one—that inner asshole that's always ready to point out your flaws and remind you of every balls-up.

Recognize Negative Thoughts

You need to recognize when this negative self-talk is happening. It's sneaky as hell, slipping into your thoughts like a pickpocket at a crowded bar. Common bullshit internal conversations include:

- ◊ "I'm not good enough."
- ◊ "She's out of my league."
- ◊ "I always mess things up."
- ◊ "No one will ever want to date me."

Once you spot these thoughts, it's time to challenge them like you're cross-examining a lying witness. Where's the evidence, counselor? Are you basing this crap on facts or just pulling fears out of your ass?

Replace that negative garbage with something positive and realistic. Instead of "I'm not good enough," try "I have unique qualities that make me valuable." Instead of "She's out of my league," think "Everyone has different preferences, and I have a lot to offer." It's not about blowing sunshine up your own ass; it's about being fair to yourself.

Challenge Negative Self-Talk

Don't even think this is some kumbaya circle where we hold hands and sing about our feelings; it's about treating yourself with the same kindness you'd offer a good friend. This is how it plays out:

When you screw up, don't berate yourself. Ask what you can learn from it. Remember, everyone has flaws and makes mistakes. You're human, not a freakin robot. Allow yourself to feel disappointed or upset. It's okay. Just don't set up camp there. Encourage yourself like you would a buddy.

"You've got this!"

"You're doing your best!"

"This is tough, but you can handle it!"

Self-compassion isn't a weakness; it's the backbone of true resilience. When you're kind to yourself, you bounce back from setbacks faster and stronger.

Progress, Not Perfection

Lastly, focus on progress, not perfection. Perfection is a myth, a moving target that you'll never hit. It's like chasing the horizon; you'll run yourself ragged and never get there. Instead, celebrate your progress and improvements.

Track your progress. Write down your achievements, no matter how small. Rather than comparing yourself to others, compare yourself to your past self, not to others. Are you better than you were a month ago? A year ago? That's what matters.

Acknowledge the effort, not just the outcome. Did you ask for that girl's number, even if she said no? That's progress. You're building courage. And, learn to appreciate the journey. Personal growth isn't a destination; it's an ongoing process. Enjoy the ride and don't be an impatient ass.

Overcoming negative self-talk is a daily battle. It's mental hygiene—like taking out the garbage—leave that shit around and it's going to fester and rot—take it out and your space is clean and healthy.

It takes practice, persistence, and a healthy dose of self-awareness. But every time you challenge a negative thought, every time you choose self-compassion over self-criticism, you're rewiring your brain. You're not just building confidence; you're building character.

This isn't just about feeling good. It's about becoming the kind of man who knows his worth isn't determined by others' opinions—the kind of man who lives life on his own terms.

First Impressions Matter

Next up we have the shark-infested waters of online dating profiles because first impressions in this game are about as forgiving as a loan shark on collection day.

Let's start with crafting a profile that doesn't make you look like a complete tool.

Crafting a Compelling Dating Profile

This is your chance to sell yourself without coming off as a used car salesman. Weep and learn:

Highlight Your Unique Shit

Everyone's got something that makes them stand out. Maybe you can do stand-up comedy while defusing bombs. Maybe you make a mean lasagna. Whatever it is, put it front and center. Don't be basic. Basic is boring, and boring doesn't get dates.

Debunking the High-Value Bullshit

This idea that you need to be a millionaire with abs of steel and a jaw that could cut glass to be "high value." It's grade-A bullshit. Here's the truth:

- ◊ **Money:** Sure, financial stability is attractive. But flashing cash like you're in a rap video? That's small cock energy. Real high value is knowing how to manage your resources, whatever they are. Splash that cash with class.
- ◊ **Looks:** You're not competing in a beauty pageant. Confidence and personality can make a 5 look like a 10.
- ◊ **Status:** Your job title isn't a personality trait. Whether you're a CEO or a janitor, what matters is how you carry yourself and treat others.

Don't completely ignore money, looks, and status—they still count for something. After all, no one's rushing to date a guy living on his mom's couch with a bank account that's perpetually in the red. But remember, real high value comes from integrity, reliability, and emotional intelligence. It's not just about your cash flow and style points; it's about being a man of your word, treating others with respect, and having your mental game on point.

Honesty is the Best Policy

Don't try to pass off that photo from five years and 30 pounds ago as current. Don't claim to be a CEO when you're really the assistant to the regional manager. Lying might get you matches, but it won't get you relationships. Be real about who you are. The right people will appreciate it.

Language Matters

Your profile isn't the place for your emo poetry or your manifesto on why all your exes are crazy. Keep it positive, engaging, and for heaven's sake, proofread. Nothing says "I don't give a crap" like a profile full of typos.

Quality Over Quantity

Your life story isn't as interesting as you think it is. Keep your profile concise. Hit the highlights. Leave some mystery. Give them a reason to want to know more.

Actions Speak Louder Than Words

Talk is cheap, and the internet is full of cheap talk. What sets you apart is your ability to walk the walk. Be consistent. If you say you'll call—call. If you make plans, keep them. Reliability is appealing as hell in a world full of flakes.

The Art of the Perfect Profile Picture

In a world where people make split-second decisions based on a single swipe, you need to stand out from the crowd. Your profile pic is like the cover of your book—it needs to make people want to read more. Here's how to nail it:

◊ **Quality Matters**

Use a high-quality photo. This isn't 1995 and your flip phone from 2005 won't cut it. If your photo is blurry, grainy, or looks like it was taken on a potato, scrap it. Invest in a decent camera or find a friend who knows their way around a DSLR.

◊ **Keep It Current**

That photo from your college glory days? Bin it. Your profile pic should be recent enough that if you met your date in person, they wouldn't think they've been catfished. Aim for something taken within the last six months.

◊ **The Solo Shot**

This is your profile, not a Where's Waldo game. Use a photo where you're the star. Group shots are for your Instagram, not your dating profile. Your potential matches don't want to play detective trying to figure out which one is you.

◊ **Framing is Key**

A good profile pic should focus on your face and upper body. Full body shots can work too, but save those for your secondary photos. Your main pic should be a clear view of your face. No sunglasses, no hats pulled low, no mysterious shadows. Let them see you.

◊ **Dress to Impress**

Wear something that makes you feel like a million bucks. This doesn't mean you need to be in a three-piece suit. But do put some effort into your appearance. Iron your shirt. Comb your hair. Look like you give a shit.

◊ **Smile, You Grumpy Nutter**

A genuine smile can make even the ugliest mug look approachable. It signals that you're friendly, open, and not a serial killer. If you're not comfortable with a full grin, try a slight smirk. Just don't look like you're plotting world domination.

◊ **Location, Location, Location**

Choose a background that adds to your photo, not distracts from it. A nice outdoor setting can work. Your messy bedroom or bathroom mirror selfie? Not so much. And for the sake of everything civilized, keep the toilet out of frame.

◊ **Action Shots**

Consider including a photo of you doing something you love. Playing guitar, rock climbing, cooking—whatever showcases your interests. It gives potential matches a glimpse into your life and provides an easy conversation starter.

◊ **The Ex Factor**

Photos with your ex are a big no. Even if you've cropped them out, we can all see that phantom arm around your shoulder. It screams "I'm not over my last relationship." The same goes for photos with kids—if they're not yours, leave them out.

◊ **The Eyes Have It**

> *Make eye contact with the camera. It creates a sense of connection with anyone viewing your profile. Plus, it shows you're confident and engaged, not hiding behind a facade.*

Your profile should be a teaser trailer for the movie that is your life. Give them enough to be intrigued, but leave them wanting more. Be honest about who you are and what you're looking for. If you're just after hookups, say so. If you're looking for a long-term relationship, put that out there. Honesty from the get-go filters out the time-wasters and attracts people who are on the same page as you.

Rejection is going to happen. A lot. Get used to it. Not everyone's going to be into you, and that's okay. It's not a reflection of your worth, it's just a mismatch. Online dating is a numbers game. The more genuine connections you attempt to make, the higher your chances of finding a good match. But don't fall into the trap of treating it like a full-time job. Set aside specific times for swiping and messaging. And don't put all your eggs in the online basket. Use dating apps as a supplement to your real-world social life, not a replacement for it.

Well, you've got the foundation now. You know what makes people tick, how to present yourself, and why your ass has been striking out. But knowing this shit is like having the keys to a Ferrari and not knowing how to drive a stick. It's time to put the pedal to the metal.

Next up, we're looking into the mind-bending world of psychological hacks. All about understanding the human psyche and using it to your advantage.

CHAPTER 2:
PSYCHOLOGICAL HACKS FOR ATTRACTION

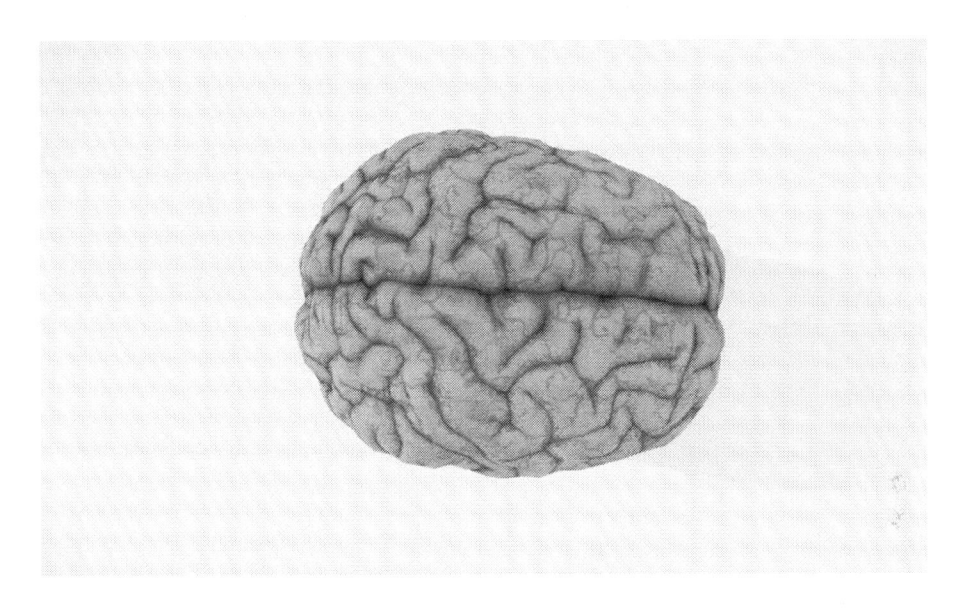

So, you want to take a look into a fresh hell of dating disasters? Matt has all the social grace of a bull in a China shop.

He's been messaging this gorgeous woman named Amber on Tinder for weeks; convinced he's got her eating out of the palm of his hand with his banter about JavaScript and the latest Marvel theories. In reality, she's about as interested as a balloon at a cactus convention.

Finally, by some miracle (or more likely, a moment of pity on her part), she agrees to meet up. Jo spends hours getting ready, even irons his favorite "May the Force Be with You" T-shirt. Real panty-dropper, that one. He shows up at the coffee shop and Amber walks in, looking like she just stepped off a runway. Jo's brain short-circuits faster than a toaster in a bathtub.

This, right here, is your masterclass in how *NOT* to interact with a woman.

So, our man Jo decides to whip out the big guns. He starts dropping "psychological facts," rambles about his coding projects, and laughs at his own jokes. By the end of this trainwreck, Amber's making excuses faster than a politician caught with his pants down, and Jo's left wondering where it all went wrong.

Guys, Jo had the right idea but damned poor execution. Understanding psychology in dating isn't about regurgitating facts like a malfunctioning Alexa.

It's about subtle application, reading the room, and not coming off like a Wikipedia page in a flesh suit.

You need to intrigue women, not have them running for the hills.

Dark Psychology: The Art of Mind-Bending

Dark psychology isn't becoming the villain in someone's story. Instead, it's recognizing the game being played all around you. It's about understanding the twisted side of human nature—you know, the part that makes reality TV so incredibly addictive. It peels back the layers of human interaction, revealing the raw, often unsettling truths about why people do what they do. Studies show that everyday people—not just career criminals or sociopaths—use dark psychology tactics, often without even realizing it (Jonason et al. 2012). That's right, your sweet old grandma might be deploying these strategies over Sunday dinner. So, understanding this stuff isn't just smart—it's downright essential if you want to navigate modern dating and social dynamics. It's your X-ray vision for bullshit, manipulation, and hidden agendas.

Now, let's boot into the holy trinity of mind-bending—and pay attention because this shit's going to revolutionize your game. It's the psychological equivalent of being the puppet master—only instead of wooden dolls, you're pulling the strings of actual people. Creepy? Maybe. Effective? You bet your ass it is. Key concepts include:

Manipulation: This is your bread and butter. It's about steering someone's behavior by recognizing the strings that are already there and using them to your advantage. We're talking joys, vulnerabilities, soft spots, cock blocks, and more. Now let me make this clear, I'm not talking about the kind of manipulation narcs and abusers use here. Your goal isn't to force anyone into doing anything. It's to simply help the woman of your desire feel comfortable enough to be her authentic self so that you both know right off the bat whether or not you're compatible. No abusive tactics bullshit—just comfort and ease of conversation. Kapish?!

Persuasion: Manipulation, just classier; the art of influence without the heavy-handedness. It's less about control and more about nudging someone in the direction you want them to go. You're presenting options in a way that makes your preferred choice seem like the obvious winner.

Ethical coercion: Now, before you start alpahing, we're not training you to be the next supervillain, this is where we keep shit real. It's about finding that sweet spot where you get what you want, but the other person doesn't feel like they've been bent over a barrel. It's not about dominating or exploiting, you're creating win-win scenarios for both of you!

Understanding Manipulation Tactics: The Three-Headed Beast

Rewiring brains, bending perceptions, and exploiting social dynamics? This isn't for the faint of heart or the morally rigid. This is not Shakespeare, brother. It's psychological warfare, and you're about to become the General.

Here's what *NOT* to do!

Emotional manipulation: Play people's feelings like a fiddle.

- ◊ Guilt-tripping: "I guess you're too busy to help me move... again."
- ◊ Gaslighting: "I never said that. You must be imagining things."
- ◊ Love bombing: Showering someone with affection until they're drowning in it.

Cognitive manipulation: This is about mind-fucking on an intellectual level.

- ◊ Framing: Presenting a situation in a way that benefits you. "It's not that I'm late, it's that I'm fashionably punctual."
- ◊ Anchoring: Setting a reference point to influence decisions. "This $5000 watch is a steal compared to the $20,000 one!"
- ◊ Scarcity: Making something seem rare or limited. "Only 5 left in stock!"

Social manipulation: Using the herd mentality to your advantage.

- ◊ Social proof: "Everyone's doing it!" (Even if 'everyone' is just your three buddies)
- ◊ Authority: Dropping names or titles to seem more credible. "As a self-proclaimed dating guru..."
- ◊ Reciprocity: Doing favors to create a sense of obligation. "I bought you a drink, so..."

Does all this sound shadier than a fart in a crowded elevator? That's because it is. Don't fall into the trap of everyone's playing this game whether they know it or not. The difference is, after reading this, you can play the game of dark psychology without being an absolute douche!

Remember, with great power comes great responsibility. Use these tactics wisely or it'll blow up in your face faster than a cheap firework. The goal here is to enhance your dating game, not turn you into a sociopath. Let's take a look at these examples again, using dark psychology ethically.

Emotional manipulation: Work people's feelings.
- ◊ "I noticed you're not feeling 100% comfortable. What can I do to help you relax?
- ◊ It was not my intention to offend you.
- ◊ Mirror the person's behaviors and body language.

Cognitive manipulation: This is about making sweet love on an intellectual level.
- ◊ Presenting a situation in a way that is a win-win. "Thanks for waiting for me. I really appreciate it!"
- ◊ Making yourself seem limited. "My schedule is pretty full this week, I can meet you at 7 on Wednesday night. How does that sound?"

Social manipulation: Using the herd mentality to your advantage.
- ◊ Social proof: Using the feel, felt, found principle. "I understand how you feel, I felt the same way. After trying it, I found that…"
- ◊ Authority: Dropping names or titles to seem more credible. "I read a study on…"
- ◊ Reciprocity: Doing favors to create a sense of obligation. "Since I chose this meeting place, where would you like to go next?"

Ethical Boundaries

Ethical considerations aren't just for Boy Scouts. They're your insurance policy against becoming a social pariah. Think of it as the difference between being James Bond and being that creepy asshole everyone avoids.

Avoid manipulation tactics that cause harm. Why? Because karma's a bitch, and so are assault charges. Plus, you're trying to find a life partner, not star in a true crime documentary. Just be transparent about your intentions. Don't promise a relationship if you're just looking to hit it and quit it. Lying might get you laid once, but honesty will keep your bed warm.

Respecting boundaries and consent isn't just about avoiding lawsuits! It's about building a reputation as a guy who gets it and quite honestly, not being a monumental asshole who is ruining it for all the other guys on the market.

Understand personal boundaries. Some people have a bubble the size of Texas. Learn to read the room, or you'll end up drinking alone. When working with boundaries, always seek explicit consent. "She didn't say no" isn't consent, genius. It's a one-way ticket to Creepville, population: you! If she said yes and then she said no, the answer is no. Nobody likes to be left hanging, but remember: "No" is a complete sentence, so stop trying to convince her otherwise. Instead, focus on being proactive and offer a few creative suggestions to keep the conversation flowing. Always be mindful of her comfort level.

> *Do not ask but suggest, always!*

Now, let's break this down further:
1. **The golden rule**: Would you be cool with someone doing this to your sister/mom/grandma? If the answer's no, don't do it. Simple as that.
2. **Consent:**
    - Step 1: Suggest
    - Step 2: Listen
    - Step 3: Respect the answer
    - Rinse and repeat. It's not rocket science.
3. **"Don't Be a Prick" principle:** Using psychology to get what you want is fine. Using it to crush someone's self-esteem or manipulate them into doing something they'll regret? That's sleazy AF.

4. **Transparency:** Be upfront about your intentions. If you're looking for a one-night stand, say so. Some people appreciate honesty more than they want a relationship.
5. **Empathy:** Try to understand where the other person is coming from. It'll make you better at reading situations and less likely to muck up.

Using these psychological tactics without ethics is like wrestling a grizzly in a phone booth. It might seem impressive, but you're bound to get mauled.

Being ethical means you're confident enough that you don't need to resort to sleazy tactics. You're not manipulating people; you're influencing them. There's a difference, and that difference is what separates the men from the boys.

Keep your moral compass handy. Not because it's the "right thing to do" (though it is), but because it's the smart thing to do.

Self-Perception: The Mirror That Doesn't Lie

How you see yourself is how the world sees you. If you think you're a pathetic loser who needs a pity stand? That's exactly what you'll project. Let me tell you, nothing kills attraction faster than desperation. You can smell that shit!

Your self-perception is your reality. If you think you're hot stuff, you'll act like it, and people will believe it. Moths are attracted to a flame, so it's time to fan the flames of your self-perception. This isn't about lying to yourself. It's about recognizing your worth and leaning into it.

Self-Validation: The Only Approval You Need

You know that rush you get when a hot woman likes your social media post? That's your brain on validation, and it's damned addictive. But it's also just as destructive.

When you rely on others for validation, you're handing over the keys to your self-worth. You're essentially saying, "Here, random stranger, you decide if I'm worthy today." Screw that for a joke!

Here's how to break free from the validation trap:

- ◊ Set your own standards. Don't let society, your mom, or that hot bartender decide what success looks like for you.
- ◊ Celebrate your wins, no matter how small. Didn't cop out when talking to that 10 at the bar? That's a win, my friend.

◊ Learn from your losses, but don't dwell on them. So you struck out. Babe Ruth struck out 1,330 times, but we remember him for the home runs.

The Power of "No"

Every rejection is a freaking gift. You read that right. When a woman rejects you, she's doing you a solid. Why? Because it wouldn't have worked out anyway, genius.

Think about it: If she's not into you, forcing it would be like trying to fit a square peg in a round hole. Rejection saves you time, money, and emotional energy. Would you rather find out now or after you've invested months?

Each rejection is a chance to refine your approach. It's not failure; it's market research.

The Myth of Universal Likability

Now, let's shatter another illusion: you don't need to be friends with everyone. In fact, trying to be universally liked is a one-way ticket to bland.

Here's why: Being polarizing is attractive. Having strong opinions means you stand for something. Not everyone will like you. Would you rather be vanilla ice cream that no one hates but no one loves, or be a damn whiskey sour that some people can't stand but others crave?

The energy you waste trying to please everyone could be spent on the people who genuinely matter.

The Rejection Reframe

Let's circle back to rejection because this is where most guys cop out. Here's how to reframe rejection so it rolls off you like water off a duck's back:

◊ **It's not about you:** Maybe she's not over her ex. Maybe she's struggling with her sexuality. Maybe she just doesn't like guys who wear Crocs. The point is, you don't know, so don't assume.

◊ **It's a numbers game:** Even MLB players only hit the ball 3 out of 10 times. You think you're better than a pro athlete?

◊ **It's practice:** Every interaction, successful or not, is making you better at this. You're leveling up, even when it doesn't feel like it.

◊ **It's a filter:** Rejection is weeding out the people who aren't right for you. Be grateful!

Once you truly, deeply value yourself, everything else falls into place. You'll attract the right people, you'll make better decisions, and you'll stop putting up with bullshit that doesn't serve you.

So, stop chasing validation like it's the last chopper out of Saigon.

Balancing Influence and Integrity

Life's about playing the long game and coming out on top without burning every forsaken bridge along the way.

Authentic relationships are like compound interests in your social life. They might start small, but they grow exponentially over time. And when it comes to using psychology to enhance communication, it isn't manipulation; it's like upgrading from dial-up to fiber optic. You're just making the connection clearer and faster. Empathy, active listening, and emotional intelligence aren't soft skills; they're your secret weapons in a world full of self-absorbed assholes.

Building genuine connections is not rocket science, but it does require some finesse. Start with authenticity, be real, but don't be an ass. Share your thoughts and feelings, but don't unleash a verbal tsunami. Remember, it's all about mutual benefit. Look for win-win scenarios and offer value before asking for anything. Be the guy who brings beer to the party, not the one who always "forgets" his wallet. Celebrate others' successes—it doesn't diminish your own and makes people want to celebrate yours.

Another key aspect is communication—speak their language. Use mirroring techniques, practice active listening, and harness the power of names. It's all about social lubrication. Don't forget empathy—it's not just for therapists and Hallmark cards. Try to understand where others are coming from, show that you get it, and use empathy to predict reactions. Knowledge is power.

Finally, don't neglect emotional intelligence. Recognize your own emotions, read the room, and manage others' emotions. Not in a manipulative way, but in a "Let's keep this shit from hitting the fan" way. Remember, IQ isn't everything.

Long-Term vs. Short-Term Strategies

Hell yes, you could use every trick in the book to get what you want right now, but that's like maxing out a credit card to buy a knockoff Rolex. You look cool for a minute, then you're screwed.

Here's why long-term thinking matters:

◊ Short-term manipulation is like a sugar high. Feels great for a moment, and then you crash hard. Think about the future you. Will you be proud of this decision in five years?

- ◊ Trust and respect are like compound interest. They take time to build, but once you have them, they keep paying dividends. Trust is earned in drops and lost in buckets.
- ◊ Sustainable connections are your social safety net. Unpredictability might be exciting, but it's hell on trust. When shit hits the fan, you want people who genuinely have your back, not a bunch of resentful puppets.
- ◊ What goes around, comes around. Every manipulative tactic leaves a mark. People might not call you out, but they remember. Ask yourself: "Is this worth potentially burning this bridge?"
- ◊ Your reputation follows you. That person you're manipulating? They talk to other people. In the age of social media, you can't just move to a new town and start fresh anymore.
- ◊ Karma's only a stitch if you are. Treat people right, and it tends to come back around. Own your mistakes. Nothing builds trust faster than admitting when you've screwed up.

The Art of Influential Integrity

You want to be influential, but you don't want to be a manipulative douchebag. Here's how you walk that line:

Be Transparent About Your Intentions

Let people know what you're after. You'd be surprised how often simply asking gets you what you want. If you can't be honest about your motives, maybe reconsider them.

Use Persuasion, Not Coercion

Present your ideas in a way that highlights mutual benefits. Give people a choice. Influence is about making your option the most attractive, not the only one.

Leverage Reciprocity Ethically

Do favors without expecting an immediate return. Play the long game. When you ask for something, make it proportional to what you've given.

Build a Reputation for Fairness

Be known for your integrity. It makes people more likely to go along with your ideas. Treat others fairly, even when it doesn't benefit you directly.

Master the Art of Negotiation

Look for win-win solutions. It's not about defeating the other person; it's about finding common ground. Be willing to walk away. Desperation is a stinky cologne.

Cultivate Charisma

Develop your authentic personal brand. Be someone people want to be around. Use storytelling to make your points. People remember stories long after they forget facts. Just don't lie

Practice Ethical Persuasion

Use logic and reason, not just emotional appeals. Be prepared to back up your claims. Bullshit might work short-term, but facts win in the long run.

Influence without integrity is like a house built on sand. This isn't just about getting laid or getting ahead. It's about building a life where you're surrounded by genuine connections, where your word means something, and where you can look at yourself in the mirror without wanting to punch yourself in the face.

The Short-Term Thinker:

For instance, Dave is all about immediate gratification. If he wants a date, he's quick to shower her with flattery and sweet talk, thinking charm alone will seal the deal. But when the charm fades and he's left with nothing but empty words, Dave's left wondering why things didn't work out.

The Long-Term Thinker:

Now, meet Alex. He plays the long game. Alex invests in meaningful conversations, shows genuine interest, and builds trust. He understands that integrity and honest connection are the real currency. His approach might not win instant admiration, but it earns lasting respect and deeper relationships. Alex's strategy isn't about quick wins; it's about building a life where his word carries weight and his connections are authentic.

In the game of life, it's not just about the cards you're dealt, it's how you play them. Play smart, play fair, and watch how the world opens up to you. Winning the game is fun, sure, but strategy and having someone to play with is where it's at!

CHAPTER 3:
CRAFTING TEXTS THAT GET RESPONSES

In this age of swipe-right romance, your texting game can make or break you faster than you can say "U up?" You might have the face of a Greek god and the body of a gym bro, but if your texts read like they were written by a horny 13-year-old with a head injury, you're history.

This chapter isn't about turning you into Shakespeare. It's about giving you the tools to stand out in her inbox like a peck pic on a nun's phone. We're talking about crafting messages that make her laugh, think, and most importantly, want to keep the conversation going.

We'll cover everything from the perfect opener that isn't "hey" to keeping the banter flowing like a river of whiskey at an Irish wedding. You'll learn how to flirt without coming off as a creep and how to seal the deal and get that date without sounding like you're trying to sell her a timeshare.

So crack your knuckles, and let's turn you into a texting titan.

The Mindset Behind Texting

Do you think you're some kind of smartphone Casanova, crafting messages smoother than a freshly waxed dolphin? Think again.

Here's the cold, hard truth that'll hit you harder than your last hangover: texting isn't your golden ticket. It's not some magical portal where you can type your way into her pants. Texting is nothing more than a glorified scheduling tool. That's it. End of story.

Let's break this down for those of you still clinging to your phones like they're life rafts in a sea of rejection. You didn't swipe right or approach her in a bar just to become her goddamn pen pal, did you? Of course not. So why the hell are you wasting hours crafting the perfect emoji combination like it's some kind of Rubik's Cube of seduction? She's not sitting there analyzing your texts. She's not swooning over your perfectly placed "lol" or your oh-so-clever pop culture reference.

Your intention when texting should be as clear as plastic heels. You're not there to entertain her, to be her therapist, or to prove you're the wittiest person this side of the Mississippi. You're there for one reason and one reason only: to set up a face-to-face meeting. Period. Full stop. End of transmission. Every text you send should have a purpose. If you find yourself mindlessly chatting about her day or her cat's digestive issues, congratulations, you've just relegated yourself to the friend zone. You might as well change your name to "Emotional Tampon" and call it a day.

And for goodness sake, stop trying to outplay her via text. This isn't chess. You can't fix a bad interaction by sending a clever meme or a perfectly timed "haha." Real attraction happens in the real world, not in some digital fantasy land where you can hide behind a screen and pretend you're not a socially awkward mess. A text is just pixels on a screen. You can't smell her perfume through your phone. You can't feel the electricity of her touch. And you sure as hell can't gauge her true interest level based on how many laughing emojis she sends. For all you know, those "haha"s could be pity laughs, and you're sitting there thinking you're the next Kevin Hart.

So here's your new mantra. Repeat after me: Schedule the date, then shut the fuck up. Use texting for logistics, not seduction. Save your charm, your wit, and your winning personality for when you're face-to-face. That's where the real magic happens. That's where you can actually show her you're not just another boring asshole with a smartphone and a thesaurus. And if you find yourself stuck in an endless text loop, unable to seal the deal? Cut your losses and move on champ. There are plenty of fish in the sea.

Now, I know what you're thinking. "But what if she's really into texting? What if she keeps the conversation going?" Well, congratulations, you've just become her entertainment for the evening. You're the digital equivalent of a dancing monkey, performing tricks for her amusement while she's probably swiping through Tinder looking for someone with the balls to actually ask her out. Women respect men who know what they want and go after it. You know what doesn't scream confidence and decisiveness? Hiding behind your phone, trying to craft the perfect message like you're writing a goddamn sonnet. You know what does? Saying, "Hey, I've enjoyed chatting. Let's grab a drink this Friday at 8. I know a great place."

Texting is a means to an end, not the end itself. It's the appetizer, not the main course. It's the trailer, not the whole damn movie. So stop treating it like it's the be-all and end-all of dating. Get off your ass, meet her in person, and show her the real you. Because at the end of the day, that's what she's interested in—not your emoji game, not your textual wit, and certainly not your ability to keep a conversation going for days without actually making a move.

Remember, Romeo, Juliet didn't fall in love with a text message. So put down the phone, grow a pair, and go meet some actual, real-life women.

4 Types of Text

Here's the lowdown on the four types of texts that'll make her phone buzz with excitement instead of dread. Pay attention.

- ◊ **Assumptions:** Stop asking for permission and start acting like you know what's up.
  - **Example:** "I bet you're the type who drinks her coffee black and judges people who add sugar."
- ◊ **Questions:** Not the boring "how was your day" bullshit. Hit her with something that'll make her brain cells dance.
  - **Example:** "If you could erase one person from history, consequences be damned, who'd you pick and why?"
- ◊ **The Flat Compliment:** Yeah, you heard me right. Sometimes, a straight-up compliment works wonders. Just don't make it creepy, dipshit.
  - **Example:** "Your taste in music is actually decent. Color me impressed."
- ◊ **The Challenge:** Light a fire under her ass. Make her want to prove you wrong.
  - **Example:** "I bet you can't go a whole day without using emojis. Loser buys drinks."

It's about the attitude, the timing, and knowing when to pull the trigger. Mix these up like a damn cocktail. Remember, texting is just foreplay for the real deal.

Components of Engaging Messages

This is the anatomy of a great text—the difference between looking like a complete dipshit and actually landing a date. So get your golden thumb ready.

The Anatomy of a Great Text

Personalization

Nobody gives a rat's ass about your day unless you're Ryan Gosling. Don't be a selfish dick, make it about them. Your job is to make them feel special like you took the time to read their profile instead of mass-swiping like a horny teenager:

Use their name. It's right there on their profile. Mention shared interests. If you both love rock climbing, lead with that. "Hey Sarah, fellow rock jockey here. Ever conquered El Capitan, or is that just a pipe dream for you too?"

Reference something from their profile. Show you've done your homework. "That photo of you skydiving is badass. Do you always seek out near-death experiences or was that a one-time thing?"

Brevity

You're not writing War and Peace here. Nobody wants to read your life story in the first message. Keep it short, sweet, and leave them wanting more. Here's the deal:

Aim for 2 to 3 sentences max. Any more and you'll look desperate. Get to the point. If you're asking them out, do it. Don't dance around it like a scared schoolboy. And, leave something to the imagination. Give them a reason to respond, not your entire biography.

Clarity

Don't be a cryptic asshole. Ambiguity might work for fortune cookies, but it's the kiss of death in texting. Be clear, be direct, and for the love of all that's holy, use proper grammar.

Use simple language. This isn't a college essay. Write like you talk (unless you talk like an idiot). Avoid vague statements. "We should hang out sometime" is weak. "Let's grab coffee at Joe's on Saturday" is strong.

Give a rat's ass and proofread. Typos are a turnoff!

Humor

Humor is like hot sauce; use it wisely and it makes everything better. Overdo it, and you'll not only leave a bad taste in their mouth but also a sting that lingers longer than you'd like.

Keep it lighthearted. You're trying to get a date, not audition for a comedy club. Use witty observations. "I see you're into yoga. I tried it once and looked like a drunk giraffe. Any tips for the flexibility-challenged?"

Playful teasing can work but tread carefully. "Oh, you're a Nickelback fan? I guess nobody's perfect. ;)"

Questions

Open-ended questions are your secret weapon. You have to give them something to work with. Open-ended questions keep the conversation flowing and show you're actually interested in what they have to say. Here's how to do it right:

Ask about their interests. "You mentioned you're into photography. What's the most challenging shot you've ever taken?" Get their opinion on something. "I'm in a heated debate with friends—is pineapple on pizza genius or sacrilege?"

Inquire about experiences. "Your profile pic looks like it was taken at Machu Picchu. What was that trip like?"

Examples of Text That Don't Suck

The first message is your opening move—it sets the tone and makes that crucial first impression.

Nail it, and you're not just another face in the crowd; you're the start of a story they want to keep reading. A killer opener shows you're not just swiping for the sake of it—you've got something to say, something worth their time. Miss the mark, and you're just background noise in their notification list. Make that first move unforgettable, because it's the difference between being a fleeting thought and the beginning of something real.

Now, let's put it all together. Here are some examples of texts that might get you a response:

The Shared Interest Opener

"Hey Alex, fellow craft beer enthusiast here. I see you're into IPAs—have you tried the new double IPA at Local Brewery? It's either liquid gold or paint thinner, I can't decide. What's your take?"

- ◊ Why it works: Personalized, shows shared interest, includes humor, and asks for their opinion.

The Profile Picture Comment

"Sarah, I've got to know—was that skydiving photo taken before or after you realized you forgot to pack a parachute? Either way, I'm impressed by your calm expression."

- ◊ Why it works: References their profile, uses humor, and indirectly compliments them.

The Hypothetical Question

"Hey Chris, quick question: If you could have dinner with any historical figure, dead or alive, who would it be and what would you order? I'm torn between pizza with Genghis Khan or sushi with Cleopatra."

- ◊ Why it works: Unique questions, show creativity, and give them an easy way to respond.

The Playful Challenge

"Alright Jamie, your profile says you're unbeatable at Mario Kart. Bold claim. I hereby challenge you to a race. The loser buys coffee. You in?"

- ◊ Why it works: References their profile, includes a playful challenge, and suggests a date in a low-pressure way.

The Current Event Tie-In

"Hey Taylor, I see you're into politics. Given the current state of affairs, if you could create a new political party, what would you call it and what would be its main platform? I'm thinking 'The Taco Tuesday Party'—free tacos for all!"

- ◊ Why it works: Shows awareness of their interests, ties in current events, includes humor and asks for their opinion.

Remember, the goal here isn't to have a full-blown conversation via text. It's to pique their interest enough to get them to agree to meet in person. Use these techniques to get your foot in the door, then seal the deal by suggesting a concrete plan to meet up. And, don't blow it by getting weird or pushy if they don't respond right away. People have lives and jobs. If they're interested, they'll respond. If not, move on. There are plenty of fish in the sea.

Your first attempts might be as smooth as sandpaper but keep at it.

Tailoring Messages: Show You're Not a Lazy Ass

Generic messages are about as exciting as watching paint dry. Personalize that shit, casanova.

When you're crafting that first message, treat their profile like it's the last damn book on Earth. Devour every detail, hunting for hobbies, passions, or anything that makes them stand out from the herd.

Then, use that intel to customize your opener. None of this "Hey, what's up?" bullshit. That's as bland as unseasoned chicken and about as likely to get a response. Instead, hit them with something specific: "So, you're into obscure 80s metal bands? Name your top three and I'll judge your taste accordingly."

Show them you've done your homework. And here's the real power move: empathy. Yeah, you heard me right. Show them you're not just another prick pic waiting to happen.

Kick things off with a statement that proves you understand their perspective: "I know getting a message from a stranger might be unexpected, but your profile intrigued me."

It's like a Trojan horse of charm—you're acknowledging the weirdness of online dating while simultaneously complimenting them.

Other solid tips that will secure you a foot in the door include:

Showing interest: Be direct, not desperate. You're a man, not a mouse. Show interest without coming off like a thirsty camel:

Direct approach: "Your style caught my eye. It's badass but in a good way. I had to come over, even if you might kidnap me."

Indirect approach: "How many guys have approached you today? None? Why's that? You seem fun."

Establishing the man-to-woman frame: Show her you're not just another "nice guy" without being a complete douche.

◊ Medium interest, high man-to-woman: "You remind me of my first crush in high school, only you're a little taller. Should I be intimidated?"

- ◊ Riskier, high interest: "Have you ever kissed a guy in the first ten seconds? No? Want to try?"
- ◊ Low-risk openers: For when you're feeling chicken. Sometimes, you need to test the waters before diving in. "What's your take on pineapple on pizza? This is a make-or-break question, by the way.

   "Are you guys best friends? You give off a 'partners in crime' vibe.

   "You two remind me of Thelma and Louise. Should I be worried about my car?"

The goal here is to start a conversation that leads to a date. Use these techniques to get your foot in the door. And for Pete's sake, don't panic if they don't respond immediately. People have lives, jobs, and maybe even better prospects than you. If they're interested, they'll respond. If not, move on.

Maintaining Momentum

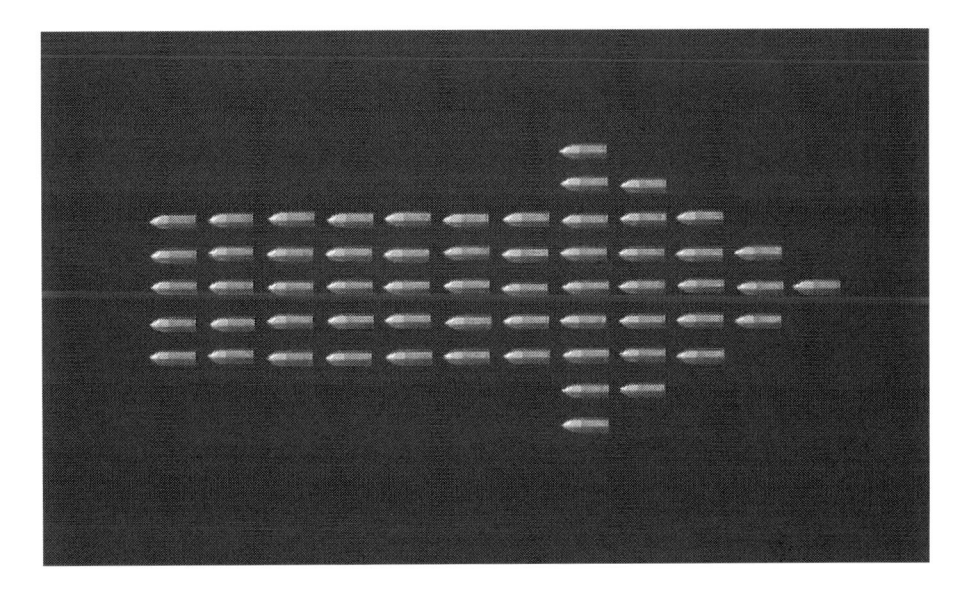

Now, let's keep that convo mojo alive and kicking and your phone screen flickering. Here's how to maintain texting momentum without falling into the boring web:

1. **Be Playful and Confident**
   - **Embrace your inner jackass:** Don't be afraid to send a quirky meme or a playful joke. Fire off a meme so ridiculous it'll make her snort coffee through her nose. Texting ain't a job interview, so stop acting like you've got a stick up your ass.
     - **Example:** "Just saw a cat wearing sunglasses. Made me think of you—cool and stylish!"
   - **Confidence over perfection:** You don't need to overthink crafting the perfect text. A confident, casual message is often more engaging.
     - **Example:** "Been thinking about our chat. What's your take on [some crazy shit]? Don't hold back, I can handle it."
2. **Keep the Convo Dynamic**
   - **Ask open-ended questions:** Ask questions that will make her brain cells dance. None of this yes/no bullshit. This keeps the conversation rolling.
     - **Example:** "If you could punch any historical figure in the face, who'd it be and why?"

- **Share fun facts or stories:** Be the most interesting gent in her inbox and bring something interesting to the table to keep things lively.
  - Example: "Did you know otters hold hands while sleeping so they don't drift apart? Meanwhile, I can't even find my keys. What's the most useless yet adorable thing you know?"

3. **Topic Roulette**
   - **Introduce new topics smoothly:** Smoothly switch gears and transition from one subject to another with ease to keep the chat fresh.
     - Example: "Speaking of cool facts, I've been trying out new recipes and experimenting with nuts. What's the most unusual dish you've ever tried?"
   - **Mix up your communication style:** Vary between casual chat, thoughtful questions, and playful banter to keep things interesting.
     - Example: "Just quit binging cat videos and watch a hilarious movie. Have you seen anything good lately?"

4. **Give a Shit About Her Shit**
   - **Dive into her passions like it's a pool full of beer:** Show some genuine interest in her passions, even if it's collecting lint. It makes the conversation feel more personal and engaging.
     - Example: "You mentioned you're into photography. Show me the craziest shot you've ever captured."
   - **Validate her feelings:** Match her energy, whether she's hyped or bummed.
     - Example: "Sounds like you had one hell of an adventure! Bet that'll be a story for the grandkids."

5. **Use Humor Wisely**
   - **Playfully tease:** Light-hearted teasing can be a great way to keep the chat fun, but make sure it's all in good spirits. Don't be a prick.
     - Example: "You claim to be a master chef? I'll believe it when I'm not dying of food poisoning."
   - **Throw down some challenges:** Nothing gets the blood pumping like a little friendly competition.
     - Example: "Bet you can't guess what song I'm blasting right now. Hint: It'd make your feet beat."

6. **Read and react to Cues**
   - **Pick up on emojis and tone:** Pay attention to how they use emojis and language. Match her vibe or she'll think you're socially retarded.
     - Example: If she's throwing hearts around like confetti, don't respond like you're sending a work email.

- **Adjust your shit based on her responses:** If she's giving you one-word answers, switch gears or abandon ship.
  - **Example:** If replies are brief, first try asking a more intriguing question or share something exciting. If you still get hit with one-worders, jump ship with respect.

7. **Plant Seeds for Future Shenanigans**
- **Dangle future plans like a carrot on a stick:** Keep her hooked for the next round.
  - Example: "Can't wait to dive deeper into [whatever crazy shit you've been discussing]—maybe over some overpriced coffee?"
- **Be clear about your intentions:** When the iron's hot, strike like Thor's hammer.
  - **Example:** "This texting shit's been fun, but let's take this circus on the road. You free this weekend?"

This ain't rocket science, but it might as well be brain surgery for some. Stay real, don't try to be someone you're not, and for Pete's sake, have some patience and tact. Don't blow up her phone like a needy teenager or she'll block your ass faster than you can say "restraining order." And, lastly, give her time to respond without hounding her like a debt collector.

CHAPTER 4: EXPERT-LEVEL TEXTING TIPS

HEY BOOTIFUL

Let's cut the bull. A bad story has no place. You need a story she'll actually want to tell her friends, instead of burying it in shame like a cat turd in a sandbox. A bloody good story. That's where you show some finesse.

You're not just some horny caveman; you're a romantic lead. Why does this matter? Because women are narrative junkies. They live for this shit. Her friends aren't gonna high-five her for banging some random dude. But if you give her a story? They'll be cooing like a bunch of drunk pigeons. "Oh my God, he's perfect! You're so lucky!"

And here's the kicker: a good story means she's more likely to come back for a sequel. You're not just a one-night stand; you're the beginning of a goddamn saga.

So start thinking like a screenwriter. Your ability to craft a narrative is the star of this show.

Alright, you narrative Neanderthals, buckle the fuck up because we're about to dive deeper into the art of not boring your date to tears with your shitty storytelling. Let's expand on this verbal voodoo and turn you into a goddamn Shakespearean savant of seduction.

The Art of Not Being a Boring Ass

Let's talk about timing. You can't just vomit your life story all over her appetizer. Storytelling is like foreplay—you gotta build up to it.

Wait for a natural opening, like when she mentions her fear of clowns, and you can smoothly transition into your tale of accidentally joining a circus for a summer. And, read the room. If she's looking at you like you're explaining quantum physics to a goldfish, wrap it up. Your story about your epic Call of Duty winning streak isn't as riveting as you think it is.

Mastering the Art of Verbal Foreplay

Now, let's talk about delivery. You're not a news anchor, so don't sound like one. Use your words like it's an instrument. Build suspense and make it exciting. If you're monotone, she might as well be reading the phone book.

The Hook, Line, and Sinker of Storytelling

Every good story needs a hook. It's like the opening line of a cheesy pick-up attempt, but less likely to get you slapped.

Start with something that grabs attention faster than free beer at a frat party. "I once woke up in a Tibetan monastery with a hangover and a pet yak." Boom. She's intrigued. Then you reel her in with the details. This is where you showcase your personality. Are you self-deprecating? Sarcastic? An eternal optimist? Whatever it is, let it shine through your story like a beacon of "This guy isn't a total waste of oxygen."

And the ending? It better be worth the build-up. A flat ending is like promising a gourmet meal and serving microwaved fish sticks. Your story should end with her either laughing, gasping, or wanting to hear more.

The Do's and Don'ts

◊ **DO:**
- Keep it relevant. If you're talking about travel and suddenly veer into your stamp collection, you've lost the plot.
- Use humor. If you can't make her laugh, at least don't make her cry. Unless it's from laughing. That's acceptable.
- Be vulnerable. Share something real. Show her you're human, not some emotionless robot pretending to be a Tinder match.

◊ **DON'T:**
- Brag. Your story about how you're God's gift to your profession is about as attractive as a herpes flare-up.
- Ramble. If your story is longer than this guide, you've gone too far. Wrap it up.
- Lie. She'll see through your bullshit faster than you can say "And then I single-handedly saved the president from ninjas."

Advanced Techniques for Storytelling

Want to take it to the next level? Here are some pro tips:

◊ **The Callback:** Remember details from her stories and weave them into yours. It shows you're actually listening and not just waiting for your turn to speak.

◊ **The Cliffhanger:** Leave a story unfinished. "And that's how I ended up in a Mexican jail. But I'll tell you how I escaped later." Boom. Now she has a reason to stick around.

◊ **The Choose Your Own Adventure:** Give her options. "So, do you want to hear how this story ends with me covered in feathers, or how it ends with me accidentally joining a cult?"

Remember, storytelling is an art, not a science. It's like jazz—you need to know the rules to break them effectively. Practice with your friends, your mom, and your therapist. Hell, practice on your dog. Just get comfortable weaving tales that don't make people want to gouge out their own eardrums.

It's about connection. It's about showing this girl that you're more than just a pretty face (or in some of your cases, a face that could curdle milk). You're sharing a piece of yourself, inviting her into your world. Don't screw it up by being as dense as a black hole.

Humor and Playfulness

This isn't just about making her giggle; it's about setting yourself apart from the sea of boring pricks blowing up her phone. And, humor is your secret weapon.

If you can make a woman laugh, you're halfway there. But here's the catch—your humor needs to be sharper than a damn samurai sword. None of that dad jokes bullshit. Puns and clever wordplay show you've got more than two brain cells to rub together. If her name's Rose, don't just say she's beautiful. Tell her she's "rose-ponsible for brightening your day." Cheesy? Maybe. Memorable? Hell yes.

Make mundane shit and blow it out of proportion. Had a rough day at work? Tell her you're pretty sure your boss is secretly plotting world domination. It's relatable, it's funny, and it shows you don't take life too seriously. Memes and gifs can be comedy gold, but use them like you would hot sauce. A little goes a long way, and too much will burn your asshole. Choose wisely, and make sure they're relevant.

Banter: The Dance of Flirtation

Banter is where boys become men and panties hit the floor. It's a delicate balance of teasing, flirting, and showing genuine interest. Get it right, and she'll be eating out of your hand.

Gentle teasing shows confidence and creates tension. If she mentions loving pineapple on pizza, playfully question her sanity. But remember, there's a fine line between teasing and being a prick. Don't cross it. Create little scenarios or inside jokes. Tell her you've decided you're both secret agents on a mission to find the world's best taco. It's stupid, but it's fun, and it creates a world that's just for the two of you.

Escalation: The Art of Turning Up the Heat

Start innocent, end dirty. Begin with playful banter about her favorite movie, and end with suggestive comments about watching it together.

But for the love of all that's holy, read the room. If she's not reciprocating, back the heck off.

The Golden Rules

- **Be authentic:** Don't try to be someone you're not. If you're not naturally funny, don't force it. Dry humor can be just as effective as being a clown.
- **Know your audience:** What makes one woman laugh might make another cringe. Pay attention to her reactions and adjust accordingly.
- **Balance is key:** Mix humor with sincerity. Show her you can be both funny and genuine. Nobody wants to date a full-time comedian.
- **Timing is everything:** Know when to crack a joke and when to be serious. If she's telling you about her dog dying, maybe hold off on the puns.
- **Practice makes perfect:** Like any skill, humor and banter improve with practice. Don't be afraid to test your material on friends first.

Now go forth and be funny, you magnificent genius.

Escalating the Interaction

Small talk is about as exciting as watching paint dry. Your job is to get past that as quickly as possible without coming off like a serial killer.

Start asking questions that actually matter. Forget "What's your favorite color?" and hit her with "What's the craziest thing you've ever done?" Get her talking about shit that means something. You gotta reciprocate. Share some of your own p stories. Show her you're human, not some robot programmed to get in her pants. And when she's spilling her guts, shut your trap and listen. Show her you're not just waiting for your turn to talk. Connect the dots between her stories and your life. It's not rocket science, it's basic human connection.

Now, start planting seeds for future hangouts. "You like sushi? I know a place that'll make your taste buds orgasm." Create anticipation for experiences. You're building a connection here, not just trying to get laid.

Reading the Room (Or the Text)

If you can't tell when she's into you, you might as well give up and join a monastery.

Is she blowing up your phone? Good sign, Einstein. Are her messages getting longer and more detailed? She's investing time in you. Don't waste it. Is she finding excuses to contact you? Congratulations, she's not repulsed by you. Trust your gut, but don't be a dumbass. If you're feeling the vibe, chances are she is too. But for Pete's sake, communicate. "I'm really into you" is a lot sexier than "Uh, do you like me?" Be ready for the hard conversations. What are you looking for? What's she after?

Don't just assume you're on the same page.

The Art of the Escalation

This isn't a sprint, it's a marathon. You're building tension, creating anticipation. Every interaction should leave her wanting more.

In your texts, start innocent and end naughty. "Good morning" can become "Woke up thinking about you" can become "Had a dream about you last night." Use innuendo like a scalpel, not a sledgehammer. Subtlety is sexy. Your words should be getting her hot and bothered. Compliment her mind, then her body. Tell her what you appreciate about her, then what you want to do to her. But remember, consent is key. Check in, and make sure she's comfortable. Nothing kills the mood faster than assuming.

Escalation is an art form. Rush it, and you'll scare her off. Go too slow, and you'll end up in the friend zone wondering what the hell happened. Find the balance, read the signs, and don't be a creep.

Let's take a quick look at practical applications, especially after discussing digital communication. Up next, a quick guide to starting engaging conversations in person, because you're gonna get to that point.

Starting Real-Life Conversations and Winning at Them

A frame isn't some fancy art shit hanging on your wall. Frames are self-fulfilling prophecies. It's your worldview, how you see yourself, and everything around you. Your frame shapes how you act, think, and interact. It's the lens you view life through, got it?

How you perceive yourself is also how other people will perceive you. If you think you're stupid, other people will perceive you as stupid. If you think you're cool, other people will perceive you as cool.

Icebreakers and Openers

The delivery of openers is essential because most men face when they deliver lines or openers. This is because:

The framework is not correct: Internalize those frameworks. Don't just copy a line. When you think you're stupid, you can't say the coolest thing in the world. But your subcommunication will tell the girl that you're not a high-value man, all right? So that's the first thing.

You can't fake a line: Often after opening, a girl will give you a shit test. For example, you'll walk up to her and say "I wanted to see if you're as cool as you're pretty." Not bad per se. She might say, 'Who are you? Why do you talk to me?" And that's a shit test.

When your frameworks are not on point, you will probably be overwhelmed. And you will think, oh my God, sorry, and you may be apologetic. But when your frameworks are on point, you might say, "Oh, I wouldn't have thought that you would have such a strong response." You can always fake a good opener. Easily possible. Okay, you can fake a good opener.

But afterward, if you get a shit test, you will fail.

Hoping for outcome: As soon as you're waiting for a certain reaction, your openers become shit. Don't worry about the outcome. Don't create expectations.

First impressions are like farts—they linger. If you want to break the ice without freezing up, pay attention because this shit might just change your dating game. Here's how to make your opener count:

Comment on something unique in their profile to show genuine interest: "Your photo at Oktoberfest has me curious—did you actually finish that massive beer stein, or did you tap out halfway? No judgment, I'd probably be under the table after two sips."

Ask a thought-provoking question to spark curiosity: "Here's a curveball for you: If you could instantly become an expert in one skill, but had to completely forget another, what would you choose?"

Share a relatable experience or observation to establish common ground: "Just tried making sushi at home. Turns out, I'm better at eating it than rolling it. My kitchen looks like a seaweed bomb went off, and my 'rolls' look like sad, fishy burritos. Any cooking tips you want to share for improvement?"

Remember, the goal here isn't to become pals for life. You're trying to build enough rapport and interest to get a second date and show you're not just an adequate texter—or at the very least, not suck on your first date.

CHAPTER 5: BOUNCING BACK FROM REJECTION AND GHOSTING

Why does getting shot down feel like a kick to the nuts? Well, let's go on a field trip to Caveman City.

Back in the day, when we were dragging our knuckles and hunting mammoths, rejection wasn't just a blow to the ego. It was a death sentence. Getting booted from the tribe meant you were bear food. So our primal brains developed this neat little trick: make rejection hurt like a "mofo" to keep us in line. Fast forward to now. We've got Netflix, Uber Eats, and indoor plumbing. You can live like a king without a single person liking your sorry ass. But guess what? Your brain's still running Caveman OS 1.0. It thinks that a hot chick turning you down at the bar is the same as being left for dead in the wilderness.

IT'S NOT. In our cushy modern world, rejection ain't shit. She says no? Big deal. The club kicks you out? Who gives a rat's ass. You'll still wake up tomorrow, chug your overpriced coffee, and drag yourself to your job like always. But your brain? That prehistoric piece of work is still screaming, "DANGER! DANGER!" every time someone looks at you funny. It's trying to save your life from a threat that doesn't exist anymore.

So here's the evolutionary takeaway: Rejection stings because we're hardwired that way. But understanding this is the first step to not letting it screw you up. Remember, no matter how hard you get shut down, you're not gonna die.

Now, let's learn how to deal with rejection like an adult.

Dealing with Rejection

We're about to dive into the art of not giving a damn when someone tells you to rock off. This isn't just about handling rejection; it's about turning that shit into rocket fuel for your dating game.

Let's get one thing straight: rejection is common in dating. Everyone, from Brad Pitt to that guy who looks like a foot, gets rejected. It's not personal, it's just life. Rejection doesn't mean you're unlovable. It just means you're not her cup of tea. And guess what? That's fantastic. Why? Because you don't want to waste your time trying to force a square peg into a round hole.

Reframing Rejection

Time to rewire that brain of yours. Rejection isn't a dead end; it's a detour to something better. Think about it:

- ◊ **It's a numbers game:** The more rejections you rack up, the closer you are to finding someone who actually appreciates your brand of bullshit.
- ◊ **Dodging bullets:** That girl who rejected you? She might be crazier than a shithouse rat. Congratulations, you just avoided a future restraining order.
- ◊ **Self-improvement fuel**: Use that sting to light a fire under your ass. Hit the gym, learn a new skill, and become the kind of guy you'd want your daughter to date.

The 10-Second Rule: You're Not Rejected, Your Behavior Is

Listen up, because this is important. When a girl rejects you, she's not rejecting YOU. She's rejecting a 10-second snippet of your behavior.

Think about it. Does she know you rescued a three-legged dog from a burning building? Does she know you volunteer at the old folks' home every Sunday? Does she know you can benchpress a small car? No, she doesn't. All she sees is a few seconds or minutes of you, probably stammering like an idiot or using some cheesy pickup line you read on Reddit. She's not rejecting your entire existence; she's rejecting that brief moment of interaction.

It's like judging an entire country based on one asshole at the airport. "Oh, this guy at O'Hare was a prick, all of America must suck." See how stupid that sounds? That's what you're doing when you take rejection personally.

Learning from the Burn

Alright, so you got shot down. Time to lick your wounds and figure out why. But remember, this isn't a pity party; it's a strategy session.

- ◊ **Play detective:** Look for patterns in your rejections. Are you coming on too strong? Are you still using pickup lines from the 90s?
- ◊ **Phone a friend:** Get some brutally honest feedback from your buddies. If they're real friends, they'll tell you when you're being a creep or if your breath could kill a small animal.
- ◊ **Implement and iterate:** Take that feedback and actually do something with it. Make a plan, stick to it, and track your progress. Celebrate the small wins, like maintaining contact without looking like a serial killer.

Rejection is going to happen. It's as inevitable as death, taxes, and disappointing Star Wars sequels. But it doesn't have to destroy you.

Remember:

- ◊ It's not you, it's your behavior (and sometimes, it's them)
- ◊ Every rejection is a step closer to the right connection
- ◊ Use it as fuel to become a better version of yourself

Now get out there and get rejected like a champ. Because the only thing worse than getting rejected is never putting yourself out there in the first place. And that, my friends, is the real failure.

Understanding Ghosting

Yup, it's dating's biggest dick move: ghosting. Why do some assholes decide to pull a Houdini on your ass?

We've got these people who'd rather crap themselves than face a little confrontation. They're so terrified of an awkward conversation, that you'd think saying "I'm not interested" would summon Satan himself. Then we've got the classic case of mismatched intentions—one's planning the wedding while the other is just trying to get laid. When that penny finally drops, some people decide it's easier to pull a Houdini than have a grown-up chat. And let's not forget the lazy asses. These worthless pricks treat dating like it's a game of Candy Crush, swiping and chatting for their dopamine hit with zero regard for the actual humans on the other end. It's a shitshow out there, gentlemen.

Spot the Difference: Token Resistance vs. Real Resistance

Before we dive deeper into ghosting, let's talk about resistance. Because if you can't tell the difference between token and real resistance, you're gonna end up either cockblocking yourself or catching a case.

Token resistance is when she's playing hard to get, testing if you've got the balls to persist. It's usually served with a side of giggles and playful vibes.

Example: "Oh, we can't go to your place... *wink wink*"

Real resistance is when she's genuinely uncomfortable or not interested. It's serious, often accompanied by body language and text tone that screams "Get me the hell out of here."

Example: "Where are we going? Seriously, dude, I want to know."

Learn to spot the difference, or you'll either miss out on willing partners or end up being that creepy guy everyone warns their friends about.

Coping with Ghosting

So, you've been ghosted. It sucks, but here's how to handle it without losing your shit:

- ◊ **Feel your feelings (but don't drown in them):** It's okay to be pissed. Ghosting is a shit move. But don't spend the next six months crying into your pillow. Feel it, then move the heck on.
- ◊ **It's not you, it's them (no, really):** Remember, ghosting says more about their character than your worth. They're the coward who can't handle a simple conversation. You dodged a bullet, my friend.
- ◊ **Focus on the living, not the ghosts:** Put your energy into people who actually give a shit. You know, the ones who respond to texts and show up for dates. Novel concept, I know.

Strategies for Moving Forward

- ◊ **The Three-Strike Rule**

    Give them three chances to respond. After that, assume they're dead (to you) and move on. No need to send that pathetic "Hey, you there?" message for the 17th time.

- ◊ **Set Your Standards**

    Make it clear early on that you expect basic human decency. If they can't handle that, they can rock right off.

- ◊ **The Ghost Buster Approach**

    If you're feeling petty (and let's be honest, sometimes we all are), send them a final message calling out their shitty behavior. "Thanks for showing me your true colors. Ghosting is for cowards. Have a nice life!" Then block their ass and move on.

Level up and turn your ghosting episode into growth. Every ghost is an opportunity to become a better, more resilient version of yourself. Here's how:

- ◊ **Self-reflection:** Take an honest look at your interactions. Were there red flags you ignored? Did you come on too strong? Learn from it, but don't beat yourself up.
- ◊ **Upgrade your bullshit detector:** Start paying attention to the signs that someone's likely to ghost. Flaky behavior, inconsistent communication, always being "busy"—these are your warning signs.
- ◊ **Diversify your dating portfolio:** Don't put all your eggs in one basket, dipshit. Keep your options open until you've had the exclusivity talk. It'll sting less when one of them pulls a disappearing act.

Ghosting sucks, but it's a reality of modern dating. Don't let it turn you into a bitter, jaded asshole. Use it as fuel to become a better, more discerning dater.

Remember:

- ◊ Not everyone deserves your time and energy.
- ◊ Your worth isn't determined by someone's inability to communicate.
- ◊ The right person won't make you question where you stand.

And if you ever feel the urge to ghost someone yourself, grow a pair and have the goddamn conversation. Be the change you want to see.

Building Resilience

Let's talk resilience, the art of getting knocked down and bouncing back like a rubber ball on steroids. This is gonna hurt so good.

Firstly, stop hanging your entire self-worth on whether Tinder Tina swipes right. You need to cultivate a life so freaking awesome that dating is just the cherry on top, not the whole sundae. Pick up a hobby that doesn't involve swiping. Learn to juggle, take up extreme ironing, whatever floats your boat. Just make sure it's something that makes you feel like a badass without needing someone else's approval.

Next, practice some self-compassion. When you screw up (and you will), don't treat yourself like you just kicked a puppy. Talk to yourself like you would to your best friend after they've had their heart stomped on. "Hey, it's okay, buddy. She wasn't worth your time anyway. Let's go get shitfaced and set her profile pic on fire." (Metaphorically, of course. We're not actually condoning arson here, you pyromaniacs.) And for crying out loud, learn to sit with your feelings without drowning in them. You got rejected? Fine. Feel that shit. Marinate in it. But don't let it consume you. Hit the gym, meditate, and journal about your feelings like a 13-year-old girl if you have to.

Find a way to process that emotional constipation without it backing up and turning you into a bitter asshole.

The Rejection Resilience Workout

Time to toughen up those fragile egos. This is the Rejection Resilience Workout, where we turn you from a whimpering puppy into a goddamn titanium-plated honey badger.

- ◊ We've got Exposure Therapy. Get your ass out there and collect rejections like they're freaking Pokemon. Ask for the most ridiculous shit imaginable—"Excuse me, can I borrow your car for a quick trip to Mars?" The more you get shot down, the less it'll feel like a bullet to the heart.
- ◊ Next, we've got the 24-Hour Rule. When rejection hits, you get one day—that's 24 hours, not a minute more—to wallow in your misery. After that, you pull up your big boy pants and move the hell on.
- ◊ Finally, there's the Gratitude Flip. For every "no" you get, find a reason to be thankful. "Thanks for not wasting my time, random Tinder chick.

Now I can focus on someone who actually deserves my awesomeness." By the time you're done with this routine, rejection will bounce off you like bullets off Superman's chest.

Mindset: Your Secret Weapon

It's time to drain your mind and fill it with something positive. Catch those negative thoughts. You know the ones: "I'm gonna die alone," "I'm too ugly/fat/short/whatever for anyone to love me." Bullshit.

Replace that crap with something more balanced. "I haven't found the right person yet, but I'm a fucking catch and it's their loss."

Practice gratitude and don't be an ungrateful dick. Every day, think of three things you're grateful for. And no, "my massive dong" doesn't count three times. Appreciate your friends who put up with your whining, your family who still loves you despite your questionable life choices and the fact that you're not a sentient potato. Lastly, visualize your ideal partner. Not just their rockin' bod, but the whole package. How do they make you feel? What kind of life do you build together? Now, here's the kicker: start embodying those qualities yourself. Want someone kind? Be kind. Want someone ambitious? Get off your ass and chase your dreams.

The "Get Rejected" Challenge: Embrace the Suck

Here's where the rubber meets the road. We're about to make you rejection-proof with a challenge that goes hand in hand with your resilience workout—because a tough mind is the ultimate shield.

8. Here's the deal: You're gonna approach 10 women and ask them if they want to sleep with you. Yeah, you heard me right. Walk up, say hi, and drop the bomb: "Do you want to sleep with me?" Your goal isn't to succeed (though if you do, congrats you magnificent specimen). Your goal is to get rejected. Hard.
9. Before each approach, write this on your arm: "My behavior is rejected, not my person." Read it out loud before and after each rejection. This isn't just some hippie-dippy affirmation bullshit. It's rewiring your caveman brain to understand that rejection won't actually kill you.

Why this works:
- ◊ **Exposure therapy:** The more you get rejected, the less it'll sting.
- ◊ **Perspective shift:** You'll see rejection isn't about you, it's about your approach.

- ◊ **Confidence booster:** Surviving this challenge will make regular approaches feel like a walk in the park.

Is this comfortable? Hell no. Will you want to crawl into a hole and die? Probably. But that's the point. You're gonna stare rejection in the face, get bitch-slapped by it repeatedly, and come out the other side stronger.

Building resilience isn't about never feeling pain. It's about taking that pain, metabolizing it, and using it as fuel to become a goddamn juggernaut of emotional strength.

Now go forth and conquer.

CHAPTER 6: TURNING TEXTS INTO REAL DATES

Let's get one thing straight: dates are not some cute little tea party where you discuss the freaking weather. They're the main event. You're there because you want to hook up now or forever, and guess what? She's there for the same reason.

Most men are so terrified of rejection that they forget why they're even on the date. You start babbling about her favorite color or some other useless bull, and before you know it, you're in the friend zone faster than you can say "blue balls." You need to keep that dating frame up like it's a tent pole in a hurricane. Show some intention. If you're not engaging in the conversation, teasing her, and getting physical, you might as well be on a date with your grandma.

And don't give me that bull about not wanting to seem creepy. As long as you're not drooling all over her like a dog, she expects you to make a move. In fact, if you don't, she'll think you're either gay or a eunuch.

So pull your head out of your ass and remember why you're there. Everything else is just window dressing.

Setting Up the First Date

Here it is, the nitty-gritty of setting up your first date; and if you don't pay attention, you might as well tattoo "Forever Alone" on your forehead.

Gauge her interest before you even think about asking her out. If she's responding to your texts with the enthusiasm of a dead fish, take the hint and move on. But if she's actually engaging, throwing some banter your way, and not treating you like a telemarketer, you might have a shot. Now, when it comes to planning, don't be a wet blanket. Choose something low-pressure that lets you talk. Coffee shops, bars, or casual restaurants are your go-to. If you want to spice it up, suggest mini-golf or bowling. Just don't propose a 12-hour hike or a visit to your mom's house, you creepy weirdo. When you ask her out, be specific. None of this "We should hang out sometime" bullshit. Give her a day, time, and place. Make it easy for her to say yes. And show some goddamn enthusiasm. If you sound like you'd rather watch paint dry, she's gonna ghost your ass.

Now, let's talk logistics. Pick a spot that's public and easily accessible. You don't want her thinking you're gonna murder her in a dark alley. Consider where she lives or works, and make sure there's parking or public transit nearby. And if you need to make reservations, do it. Show some initiative. But here's where it gets real:

- ◊ First off, be 30 minutes early and approach other girls before your date shows up. This isn't so you can hedge your bets. It's to get you in the zone. Practice your game, get your energy up, and remind yourself that you've got options. Just make sure your date doesn't see that.

- ◊ Next, dress like you give a shit. Not what you think she wants to see, but what makes you feel like a boss. If you're not feeling yourself, she sure as hell won't be either.

- ◊ And for the love of all that is holy, have some basic hygiene. Shower, shave, brush your teeth, and pop a breath mint. You'd be amazed how many dumbasses show up to dates smelling like a dumpster fire. Don't be that guy.

- ◊ Lastly, get your blood pumping before the date. Hit the gym, ride your bike, or even just take a brisk walk. It'll energize you and keep you from acting like a nervous wreck.

The day before, send a quick confirmation text. Something like, "Looking forward to seeing you tomorrow at 7 at Joe's Bar." Simple, direct, and it shows you're not flaky.

Remember, you're not there to make a new bestie or discuss the weather. Keep that hook-up frame up, show some intention, and be a man.

The Soft Close

It's time to talk about closing. If you screw this up, you might as well hand in your man card and resign yourself to a lifetime of lonely nights and carpal tunnel syndrome.

Closing is the Holy Grail of your texting interaction. Closing isn't just about getting her number; it's about asking for it in real life, not through online chat. You can charm her panties off all night, but if you can't seal the deal, you're just a clown performing for free. Here's how to not be a total screw-up:

- ◊ **Timing Is Everything**
  - Close when she's on a high, not when she's crying about her dead goldfish
  - Look for signs: Is she laughing? Is she touching you? Is she not looking at you like you're a piece of shit on her shoe? That's your cue, Romeo, ask for her direct number.
- ◊ **Always Be Closing (ABC)**
  - Never, and I mean NEVER, leave an interaction without trying to close
  - If you're not closing, you're just jerking off socially. Grow a pair and make your move
- ◊ **Don't Be a Hit-and-Run Artist**
  - Got her number? Great. Now don't run away like you just stole her purse
  - Stick around for a bit. Show her you're not just some number-collecting creep
  - Every second you stay after closing builds more comfort. Use it
- ◊ **Suggest, Don't Beg**
  - "Can I maybe, possibly, pretty please have your number?" Hell no. You're not Oliver Twist asking for more gruel
  - Pull out your phone and say, "Let's exchange numbers." It's not a question, it's a statement

The soft close is about being smooth while still getting what you want. Here's how it goes down:

You've been chatting her up, she's laughing at your lame jokes, and you can practically smell the attraction. Now's your moment, Casanova. Say something like, "Hey, this has been great. We should continue this over coffee sometime." Then, without missing a beat, whip out your phone like it's the most natural thing in the world. If she hesitates, don't panic. Keep it cool. Say something like, "No pressure, just thought it'd be fun to chat more when we're not surrounded by the local village idiots." Then change the subject. You're planting a seed, not trying to uproot a bloody oak tree.

Closing isn't just about getting a number. It's about setting up the next interaction. So don't just collect digits like some kind of number hoarder. Make a plan. "How about we grab that coffee on Thursday?" Be specific, be confident, and be memorable.

And here's a pro tip, for you amateurs: Always, and I mean always, send a follow-up text that same night. Something simple like, "Great meeting you. Looking forward to Thursday." This cements you in her mind and shows you're not some dodgy asshole looking for ass.

Navigating the First Date

If you can't handle the first date, you can expect a shitstorm and might as well call it a day. But there's no need to be a freaking trainwreck.

A good place to start is to look like you actually care about what you look like. Remember, clean, well-fitting clothes that don't make you look like you just crawled out of a dumpster, and your breath shouldn't be able to strip paint off walls. Get a haircut while you're at it. Looking like Chewbacca's inbred cousin isn't going to win you any points.

Now, don't be a flaky dumbass—late is never fashionable. Show up early. If you're on time, you're already late in this game. And if you're running behind because you can't manage your time like a functional adult, at least have the decency to text her. Don't leave her hanging, wondering if she's been stood up.

When you're actually face-to-face, act like you've got more than two brain cells to rub together. Make eye contact. Her eyes are up there, not on her chest. And for the love of masculinity, put your damn phone away. Instagram can wait. Show her you're actually present and not some social media zombie.

The Art of the Follow-Up IRL

So you've nailed the texting game, met for a quick catch-up to see if this shit will work, and you've successfully landed an actual date—congratulations! Now, how do you keep that conversational mojo going once you're face-to-face for an extended period of time? It's time to shift gears from the digital chatter and quick meets to real-life, full-on dialogue. Yes, it's IRL!

Most gents freeze up like a deer in headlights, thinking they need to suddenly become Shakespeare to keep her interested. Newsflash: your verbal skills aren't the problem. You can chat for hours with your mom or your bros, right? The real issue: you've put this chick on a pedestal. You're so busy trying to impress her, you're overthinking every damn word. It's like your brain's running a bloody quality control check on every thought. "Is this cool enough? Will she like me if I say this?" And that gents, is how you end up sounding like a boring asshole.

The secret? Stop giving a rat's ass if what you're saying is "Good enough" for her. I've got 20 different thoughts bouncing around my skull right now—my phone, my charger, this canvas on my wall. When I'm engaged in a real-life conversation with a woman, I don't filter that shit. I just let it flow.

So here's your homework: stop qualifying your thoughts. Once you drop this need to impress, you'll become a goddamn conversational Jedi. It's not about having the perfect thing to say. It's about not giving a shit if it's perfect. But, to not give a shit you have to know how to play the game. This is what we call maintaining momentum 101, a.k.a… Don't be a boring ass!

Keeping the Conversation Rolling

Breaking the ice without being a total creep is an art form, so pay attention. Compliment something specific about her. "Nice eyes" is a weak sauce. "That necklace really brings out your eyes" shows you're actually paying attention.

And, try to find some humor in your surroundings. If you can't crack a joke about the situation, you're about as entertaining as watching paint dry. When it comes to questions, don't be lazy. Ask things that can't be answered with a simple yes or no. "What's your passion?" are leagues better than "Do you like your job?" Get her talking about herself. People love that shit, and it takes the pressure off you to not sound like a complete moron.

But don't just interrogate her like some discount detective. Share your own shit too. Offer up some info about yourself, just don't monologue. It's a conversation, not your one-man show. Find some common ground. If you both love dogs, you've hit the jackpot.

Just don't fake it. She'll smell your bullshit a mile away, and then you're really screwed.

The Art of IRL: Show You Give a Damn

You've got her there and you've got her talking, great. Now don't screw it up by letting the conversation die. Remember, people love talking about themselves. Give them the spotlight and watch them shine. Here's how to keep that ball rolling:

Ask follow-up questions like your life depends on it: "So you climbed Kilimanjaro? That's badass. Any close calls with man-eating lions, or just altitude sickness?"

Dig deeper: "You mentioned you're into urban exploration. What's the creepiest abandoned place you've ever stumbled into? Any ghost sightings or just tetanus risks?"

Share your shit. But make it relevant: But don't just sit there nodding like a bobblehead. Share your shit, but keep it relevant. Tell a story that doesn't suck. Bring something to the table:

Tell a story that doesn't suck: "Your tale of getting lost in Tokyo reminds me of the time I ended up in a sumo wrestler's changing room by mistake. Let's just say I saw more man-thong than I ever wanted to."

Keep it relevant: If they're talking about their pet tarantula, don't start yapping about your grandma's dentures. Stay on topic.

Switch it up: Keep 'em on their toes: Talking about one thing for too long is like eating the same meal every day—it gets old fast. Mix it up:

Introduce new topics smoothly: "Speaking of bizarre foods, have you heard about that restaurant that serves only dishes inspired by famous movie scenes? I'm torn between the 'Lady and the Tramp' spaghetti and the 'Pulp Fiction' Big Kahuna Burger."

Ask for their opinion: "I've been binge-watching true crime docs lately. Am I becoming paranoid, or just well-prepared for the zombie apocalypse? What's your take?"

The hypothetical: Get their imagination going: Pose fun, imaginative scenarios: "If you could have dinner with any three people, dead or alive, who would you choose? And more importantly, what would you serve?"

Spark some friendly competition: Propose a lighthearted bet or challenge. "I bet I can guess your favorite ice cream flavor in three tries. If I win, you owe me a scoop. If you win, I'll buy you two."

Find common ground: Use movies, TV shows, or music to connect. "Your profile pic gives me strong 'Parks and Rec' vibes. Are you more of a Leslie Knope or a Ron Swanson?"

Recognizing and Responding to Interest: Don't Miss the Signs

Read the room, Sherlock! Not everyone's going to spell out their interest for you. You're going to need to learn to read between the lines. For instance:

- ◊ **Her: "Do you say that to all girls?"**
  - You: "Oh absolutely, you're number 225 today. I'm going for a world record."
  - Don't get your panties in a twist. Show her you can take a joke and dish it right back.
- ◊ **Her: "You're such a player."**
  - You: "Guilty as charged. I'm actually the president of the Players Association. Want an autograph?"
  - Own that shit. Make it so ridiculous she can't help but laugh.

- ◊ **Her: "Do you do this often?"**
  - You: "I don't know, do you ask that question often?"
  - Flip the script, you clever dick. Make her qualify herself to you.
- ◊ **Her: "You're just acting like you're cool."**
  - You: "Damn, you caught me. I'm a nervous wreck. Hold me?"
  - Agree and amplify. Make it so absurd she'll feel stupid for even suggesting it.
- ◊ **Her: "I'm not that easy to get."**
  - You: "Good, I love a challenge. Shall we arm wrestle for it?"
  - Don't chase. Make it a game where you're both playing.
- ◊ **Her: "All men are assholes."**
  - You: "True. We have a secret club and everything. The initiation involves puppies and kittens, though, so it balances out."
  - Don't throw other men under the bus, you backstabbing coward. Make light of it instead.

The goal is to be as unshakeable as a drunk uncle at a wedding. Don't get defensive, don't explain yourself, and don't start sweating like you're in a sauna.

Length matters: If they're talking the back legs off a donkey, they're into you. If you're getting one-word answers, they're not interested or you're boring as hell.

Enthusiasm is key: "OMG, I love that band too!" is interesting. "Cool" is not. Learn the difference.

Mirror, mirror on the wall: Monkey see, monkey do. Match their style: If they're throwing around jokes like confetti, feel free to unleash your inner joker artist. If they're all business, keep it classy. No one-liners for you, funny guy.

The future plans tease: Casually mention potential future activities: "I've been meaning to check out that new escape room. Sounds like the perfect test for our problem-solving skills, don't you think?"

Spot the green light: Some people are about as subtle as a brick to the face. Others, you need a microscope to spot their interest. Here's what to look for:

> *They ask about your schedule:* "What's your week looking like?" Translation: "When can I see you?"

> *Or, if they're telling you about their childhood trauma, they're either very interested or need therapy. Possibly both. They use "we" language: "We should try that new restaurant sometime." Congrats, you're now a "we".*

Use these techniques to keep the conversation engaging, but don't drag it out forever.

Don't Screw Up the Logistics

Venue changing is crucial, but if you don't know your ass from your elbow when it comes to your city, you're screwed.

Know your surroundings like the back of your hand. Have a food spot in mind, because nothing kills the mood like a hangry date. Know where the good bars are, and no, your local dive where everyone knows your name doesn't count. Have a game plan, for Pete's sake. Your place better be close or have easy transport. Uber exists for a reason, use it. If you're stumbling around like a lost puppy trying to figure out where to go next, she's gonna bail.

Logistics are key. If you can't smoothly transition from one spot to another, you might as well pack it in and go home to your hand. Always have a backup plan. Shit happens. That trendy bar might be packed, or that cool restaurant might be closed. Be ready to pivot without looking like a deer in headlights.

Lastly, read the room. If she's into it, great. If she's looking for an escape route, don't force it. Better to end on a high note than drag it out like a bad sitcom.

And if you end up like a bad sitcom, well, there's always cats. Lots and lots of cats.

Post-Date Communication

Alright, you can either rock post-date communication or invest in a lifetime supply of lotion and tissues. You've got options.

◊ **Don't Be a Ghost**

You need to follow up after the date. Don't wait three days like some outdated bullshit advice from your grandpa's era. Send a text that night or the next day. Something like, "Had a great time watching you destroy that burger. Didn't know I was on a date with a competitive eater." Show her you were actually paying attention and not just staring down her shirt the whole time. Give her a compliment that isn't about her physical appearance. "Your passion for rescuing three-legged dogs is actually pretty badass" is way better than "Nice ass." Show her you've got more depth than a kiddie pool.

◊ **Keep the Conversation Rolling**

Don't let the conversation die. Ask her something thought-provoking based on what you talked about. If she mentioned loving true crime podcasts, hit her with a "So, which serial killer do you think you could take in a fight?" Keep it light, keep it fun, and keep it going.

- **Planning the Next Date (Because You Somehow Didn't Fuck Up the First One)**

    Now, if by some miracle she hasn't blocked your number, it's time to plan the next date. Don't just suggest "drinks." If she mentioned loving art, suggest a street art tour followed by creating your own graffiti masterpiece (legally, you vandal). Show her you've got some creativity. Offer options, but don't overwhelm her with a fucking novel of suggestions. "I was thinking we could check out that new escape room, or if you're feeling adventurous, there's an ax-throwing place that just opened up. Your call on whether you want to solve puzzles or unleash your inner Viking." Let her have a say.

- **Staying on Her Radar Without Being a Stalker**

    In between dates, keep the line open. Send her memes that aren't complete shit. Share an article about something she's interested in, showing you've got more going on upstairs than just fantasies about her. But don't blow up her phone like a needy teenager. Quality over quantity. As things progress, you can start diving into deeper conversations. But remember, this isn't your therapist's couch. Keep it balanced between serious and fun. "So, what's your stance on the existential dread of human existence? Also, have you seen this video of a cat riding a Roomba?"

- **Don't Be Flaky**

    If you say you're gonna do something, bloody do it. If you promised to send her that playlist of obscure 80s synth-pop, deliver it faster than a pizza guy hoping for a big tip. Consistency is key. Show her you're reliable. Express your enthusiasm about where this might be heading, but don't come on stronger than body odor. "I'm really looking forward to seeing where this goes. You're like a mystery novel I can't put down, except with better jokes and less murder." Show her you're invested without planning your wedding after two dates.

Remember, you're building something here. It's like constructing a house of cards, except the cards are your fragile ego and her rapidly dwindling patience. Don't screw it up by being too eager, too aloof, or too much of a dumbass.

CHAPTER 7: VIDEO COURSE INTEGRATION

Strap in because your dating life's gonna become so hot, it'll make the sun look like a goddamn ice cube. Welcome to the video course, that's gonna turn you from a dating zero to a certified hero.

You've got the book, great. But this video course? It's like injecting that knowledge directly into your eyeballs. We're talking visual demonstrations that'll make these concepts stick like gum on a stripper's heel. You'll see real people—not actors, not models, but genuine humans—putting these techniques into action. We've dragged dating experts out of their lairs to share their hard-earned wisdom. These are the folks who've been in the trenches, take the hits, and come out the other side with more notches on their bedposts than a lumberjack's ax handle.

The endgame here is simple: we're going to rewire your brain. We're not just aiming to boost your confidence; we're going to launch it into the stratosphere. You'll go from "Who's that guy?" to "WHO is THAT guy?" Each video is designed to fit into your life, no matter how chaotic. We're talking 46 modules, each one a concentrated shot of dating espresso, guaranteed to wake up your love life.

What We're Jamming Into Your Skull

We're covering everything from A to Z in the dating alphabet. Here's a taste of the feast we're laying out:

- ◊ "Approach Your First Women"—Because you can't win if you don't play, champ.
- ◊ "Who is Getting All the Girls Out There"—Spoiler: It's about to be you.
- ◊ "Strength of Frame"—How to be unshakeable without being an unbearable prick.
- ◊ "How to Feel Good Enough"—Spoiler: You already are, we're just going to make you believe it.
- ◊ "Looks"—Maximizing your genetic lottery ticket, whether you hit the jackpot or got the consolation prize.
- ◊ "Conversation"—The art of talking your way into her mind, heart, and maybe more.
- ◊ "Hook Point"—Learn to reel her in like a master fisherman of attraction.
- ◊ "Closing"—Sealing the deal without feeling like a used car salesman.

But there's more! We've got modules on "Shit Tests" (because women will test you, and you need to be ready), "Hot Girls Reality" (it's not what you think, trust us), and "Pulling 1 & 2" (a two-part masterclass in sealing the deal).

Each of these topics takes what you learned in the book and supercharges it. We're not just telling you what to do; we're showing you how to do it, when to do it, and why it works. It's time to take all that theory and turn it into cold, hard practice.

Bonus Shit That'll Make You Unstoppable

Because we're feeling generous (and because we want you to succeed so badly it hurts), we're throwing in some extras that'll give you that extra edge:

1. Q&A sessions where you can ask the questions that keep you up at night. Trust us, we've heard it all, and we're here to clear up every last doubt.
2. Downloadable cheat sheets that distill each lesson into a format so simple, that even your drunk self can understand it.
3. Access to a private community of men on the same journey. Iron sharpens iron, and in this forge, we're crafting freaking legends.

The Nitty-Gritty

You've already got the book—that's a solid start. But the real magic happens in the video course. Think of it as the book on steroids.

Every piece of knowledge gets translated into practical, real-world action with visual demonstrations. And we're not just talking theory here—these are real people, not actors, showing you exactly how it's done. We've assembled top experts in the dating field, individuals who've experienced the ups and downs, and they're sharing their hard-earned wisdom with you.

If you've ever found yourself paralyzed in the middle of a conversation, not knowing what to say, or lacking the confidence to approach the woman you're interested in—this course is going to change that. You're going to rewire how you think, act, and feel in these situations. You'll transition from feeling stuck to becoming someone who approaches, connects, and builds genuine attraction effortlessly. Let's dive into what this course offers. You'll learn how to confidently approach women without hesitation, master the art of conversation so that you never run out of things to say, and attract not just any woman—but the right woman. You'll cultivate a mindset that radiates confidence, not just for a night, but for life.

This course includes 46 highly focused modules, each one designed to fit into your busy schedule. You'll gain the tools to overcome all the common obstacles that have held you back—whether it's starting a conversation, keeping it flowing, or knowing when and how to close the deal. You'll understand the psychology behind attraction and how to apply it in real life, without ever feeling like you're putting on an act.

But that's not all. We're also including bonus content, featuring live Q&A sessions with the experts, so you can pose your specific questions and receive real-time answers. You'll also get downloadable cheat sheets to keep the key lessons fresh in your mind and access to a private community of like-minded men who are on the same journey. Imagine the power of having a group that supports and sharpens your skills as you evolve.

This is your chance to break free from confusion and uncertainty. Take the next step to becoming the man who effortlessly attracts women because he's confident, self-assured, and authentic. Grab your phone, scan the QR code, and get access to all this content right now. Don't let this opportunity pass—your dating transformation starts today.

You've already made it this far, so don't stop now. Take action, dive into the course, and start living the dating life you've always wanted. It's time to elevate your life.

How to Use the Video Course

This video course isn't just some fancy add-on to make the book look pretty. It's the nitrous oxide to your dating engine. Here's how to use it without fucking it up royally:

The first rule of Video Course Club: Follow the damn order. Don't just randomly click on videos like a monkey on meth. We've laid it out for you like a trail of breadcrumbs. After each chapter, click on the corresponding videos.

For example: Chapter 1, Video 1. Chapter 2, Video 2 and 3. See the pattern?

But here's where it gets interesting. Life's gonna throw curveballs at you. You'll get rejected, ghosted, or worse. When that happens, don't crawl into a hole with a bottle of Jack. Revisit the videos. They're not one-and-done; they're your personal pep talk on demand. After each video, you've got homework. Yeah, I know, homework sucks, but suck it up, buttercup. We've got reflection questions that'll make you dig deeper than your ex's Facebook profile. How does this apply to your life? What would you do in that situation? It's not rhetorical. Actually, answer them.

We want you to practice these skills. Go out there and try this shit. Then come back and tell us how it went. Bombed spectacularly? Great, watch it again and figure out where you screwed up.

We've sprinkled examples and case studies throughout the videos like Easter eggs. Find the connections. It's all interconnected.

Maximizing Learning:
Because Your Brain Needs All the Help It Can Get

We're hitting you with a triple threat here: visual, auditory, and written content. Why? Because your brain needs all the help it can get to absorb this shit. Some of you learn by seeing, some by hearing, and some of you need it beaten into you with written words. We've got you covered.

Set up your learning space like it's a goddamn shrine to your future love life. No distractions. No interruptions. Just you, the content, and your burning desire not to die alone surrounded by cats. Take notes, pause the video, and rewind if you need to. Hell, do interpretive dance if it helps you remember. We're not running a race here. Better to take it slow than to rush through and still be clueless at the end.

Can't figure out how to work a video player? For Pete's sake. Here's a crash course:

- ◊ If it's buffering, check your internet. Maybe stop downloading porn for five minutes.
- ◊ Playback issues? Try turning it off and on again. Works for relationships too.
- ◊ Still stuck? There's customer support. Use it. That's what they're paid for

Don't let technical difficulties cockblock your journey to romantic competence. If you can figure out how to unhook a bra, you can figure out how to play a damn video.

This isn't a one-night stand of learning, it's a long-term relationship. Schedule regular refreshers. Set reminders on your phone. "Hey, time to rewatch Chapter 3!" Your dating life is a journey, not a destination. Use these videos like a shot of espresso for your love life.

When you're feeling down, unmotivated, or like the dating world is a dumpster fire (it is, but that's beside the point), come back to these videos and the book. Let them remind you why you started this journey and why you're a catch.

The Method to Our Madness

There's a reason we've structured this course the way we have. It's designed to build on itself, like Lego. The videos reinforce and expand on the book's content. It's not just repetition; it's repetition with a purpose.

Watch these like you're studying game film before the big match. Because guess what? Dating is a game.

Here's your game plan:

1. Read a chapter
2. Watch corresponding videos
3. Do the call to action
4. Go out and practice
5. Come back, rewatch, reassess
6. Rinse and repeat until you're a dating god

It's about becoming the kind of person who naturally attracts others. It's about confidence, charisma, and not being a total trainwreck in social situations.

We've handed you the dating equivalent of a lightsaber. But even Luke Skywalker had to practice before he could take on Darth Vader. This is your training montage, Rocky. Your Mr. Miyagi moment. Don't half-ass this. Full-ass it. Commit to the process. Trust the system. It's worked for thousands of hopeless cases before you, and it'll work for you too if you put in the effort.

CHAPTER 8: TEXT TEMPLATES THAT WORK

It's time to talk about the secret weapon in your digital dating arsenal: message templates. You know, those pre-written messages designed to make you sound like you have more than two brain cells when you're trying to slide into someone's DMs?

Yup, we're about to turn you into a smooth operator.

Now, before you start whining about how "real men don't use templates," let me stop you right there. Real men use every goddamn tool at their disposal to get the job done. And in this case, the job is not looking like a complete ass-hat.

The Benefits of Using Templates: Your Shortcut to Not Sucking

Most men have the conversational skills of a drunk sloth when it comes to talking to women online. That's where templates come in, my friend. They're like training wheels for your attempts at flirtation. Here's why you need them:

Time-Saving Magic

Templates save you from staring at your phone like a deer in headlights, trying to come up with something cleverer than "hey."

With a solid set of templates, you can overcome that pesky writer's block faster than you can say "swipe right." No more agonizing over every word like you're defusing a bomb. Just pick a template, tweak it, and boom—you're in the game. And let's be real, you're not just talking to one woman, are you? Templates let you juggle multiple conversations without losing your mind. It's like having a personal assistant for your love life, minus the judgmental looks.

Boosting Your Response Rates Like a Boss

These aren't just random bullshit thrown together by some sexually frustrated intern. These templates are engineered to get responses faster than free beer.

They incorporate proven storytelling techniques that'll have her hanging on enough to write back. Good templates give you conversation starters that actually get answered, not just left on read. They include calls to action that give her something to respond to, instead of leaving her wondering why the hell you bothered messaging her in the first place. They help you avoid those classic fuck-ups that normally send women running for the hills. No more talking about yourself like you're God's gift to dating. No more boring her to tears with your mundane day-to-day bullshit.

These templates are designed to spark curiosity and keep her intrigued. It's like having a wingman in your pocket, minus the tequila breath.

Structure for You

Coming up with original, witty messages for every match is about as appealing as a root canal. Templates give you a jumping-off point. They provide the bones of a good message, and it's your job to put some meat on them.

Think of templates as cheat codes for dating apps. They give you the structure and the key elements that make a message work. Your job is to take that structure and make it your own. It's like learning chord progressions in music. Once you know the basics, you can start to improvise without sounding like a cat in heat.

Personalizing Templates: Don't Be a Lazy Prat

Now, before you go copy-pasting these bad boys like there's no tomorrow, the goal isn't to sound like a chatbot with a libido. It's to give you a starting point so you can craft messages that don't make you sound like a complete tool.

Highlight Something Specific

Do you know what women love? Being seen as actual human beings and not just another face in your endless scroll of potential hookups. Crazy concept, I know.

So when you're using a template, make sure you're highlighting something specific from their profile. Did she mention she's into rock climbing? Don't just say "Oh, cool, you like rock climbing." Dig deeper, you simpleton. Say something like, "I see you're into rock climbing. Let me guess, you're the type who'd scale El Capitan in flip flops just for the hell of it?" Show her you actually read her profile and aren't just mass-messaging every woman within a 50-mile radius.

Reference a shared hobby, hometown, or some quirky fact that stood out to you. Explain what caught your attention and why you'd like to learn more about it. It's not rocket science, but it does require you to engage your brain for more than two seconds.

Inject Your Personality

Templates are a starting point, not the finish line. You need to inject your own personality into these messages. Otherwise, you'll sound about as authentic as a Rolex bought from a guy in a trench coat.

Rephrase those generic lines in your own voice. If the template says "I couldn't help but notice your love for travel," and that sounds about as natural coming from you as Shakespearean English, change it up. Maybe something like "So, I see you're a globe-trotter. What's the weirdest thing you've eaten on your travels?" is more your speed.

And for the love of all that's holy, use your sense of humor. Assuming you have one. If you've been chatting with her for a bit, throw in an inside joke or a playful tease. Show her you're paying attention and not just robotically working your way through a script.

Polish That Turd

Before you hit send, take a second to proofread your message. Nothing kills attraction faster than looking like you flunked third-grade English. Double-check your spelling, make sure your grammar isn't atrocious, and make sure you're hitting the right tone.

You want a balance of information and intrigue. Give her enough to be interested, but leave her wanting more. Leave her curious enough to write back.

The Art of Template Mastery: Becoming a Smooth Operator

Now that you've got the basics down, it's time to level up your template game. This isn't just about having a few pre-written messages. It's about developing a system that turns you into a smooth operator.

Building Your Template Arsenal

Start by creating a diverse range of templates for different situations. You need openers, follow-ups, date suggestions, and the works.

Think of it like building a wardrobe. You wouldn't wear the same shirt every day, so don't use the same template for every situation. Create templates for different types of profiles. Got a match who's big into travel? Have a template ready to go that can easily be customized for world adventurers. See someone with a quirky hobby? Prepare a template that shows genuine curiosity about unique interests.

The key here is variety. The more templates you have, the less likely you are to sound repetitive or boring. And trust me, in the world of online dating, boring is a death sentence.

Adapting on the Fly

Here's where the real magic happens. As you use these templates more and more, you'll start to internalize their structure and flow. You'll begin to understand why certain phrases work and others fall flat.

Eventually, you'll find yourself improvising more and relying on strict templates less. It's like learning a language. At first, you need to memorize phrases. But as you get more comfortable, you start forming your own sentences. This is the goal, gentlemen. To get to a point where you can craft a killer message on the fly, using the principles you've learned from your templates.

It's not about becoming dependent on pre-written text. It's about using templates as training wheels until you can ride on your own.

Avoiding the Template Trap

Now, a word of warning: don't become a template zombie. If you're copy-pasting the same message to every match, congratulations, you've become the very thing we're trying to avoid—a boring, unoriginal douchebag.

The whole point of templates is to give you a foundation to build on, not a crutch to lean on. If you find yourself unable to send a message without consulting your template library, it's time to take a step back and reassess.

The goal is authentic communication. Templates are just a tool to help you get there. They're not a replacement for genuine interest and conversation skills.

Continuous Improvement: Stay Sharp or Get Left Behind

The world of online dating is constantly evolving, and your approach needs to evolve with it. What worked last year might fall flat today. That's why you need to be constantly refining your template game.

Pay attention to which templates get the best responses. Analyze why some messages work better than others. Are certain phrases resonating more? Are some types of questions getting more engagement? Use this information to continually update and improve your template arsenal.

Stay current. Reference recent events, popular culture, or trending topics in your templates. Nothing says "I'm an out-of-touch loser" like using dated references or memes that were cool five years ago.

The Endgame: Beyond Templates

Templates are not meant to be a permanent solution. The end goal is to become so comfortable and confident in your communication that you don't need templates anymore.

> *Understand the psychology behind effective messages. Learn how to create intrigue, how to balance humor and sincerity, and how to show genuine interest without coming across as desperate. Eventually, you'll find that crafting engaging messages becomes second nature. You'll be able to look at a profile and immediately know how to start a compelling conversation. That's when you've truly mastered the art of online dating communication.*

Use these templates as a starting point. Learn from them.

CONCLUSION

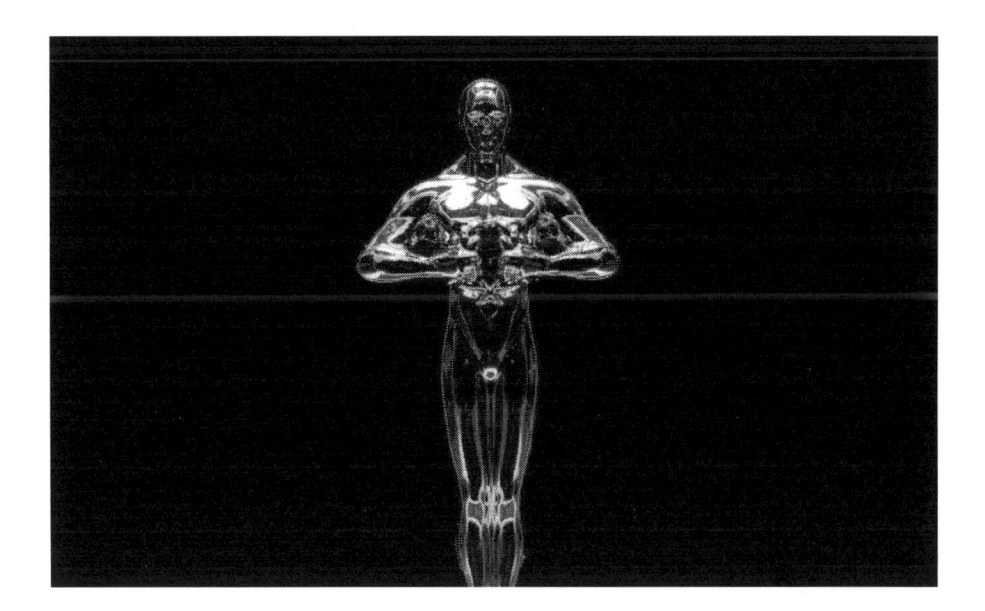

Before you run off to unleash your newfound powers on the unsuspecting dating world, let's have a little heart-to-heart.

First things first: If you think you've magically transformed into God's gift to women just by reading this book, you're in for a rude awakening. This isn't some Harry Potter bullshit where you wave a wand and suddenly become irresistible. No, my friend, this is just the beginning of your quest from zero to hero in the dating game. The moment you stop improving is the moment you start sliding backward. The dating landscape is constantly evolving, and if you're not keeping up, you're getting left behind.

So how do you stay ahead of the curve? Simple. You practice, you adapt, and you never stop learning.

Every interaction is a chance to refine your skills. Bombed a conversation? Good. Analyze that shit like it's the Zapruder film. Figure out where you went wrong and adjust your approach. Got a positive response? Even better. Dissect that success and replicate it. And, don't just limit yourself to dating apps. Take these skills out into the real world. Talk to women in bars, coffee shops, bookstores—hell, strike up a conversation with the cute cashier at your local supermarket (but keep it classy). The more you practice, the more natural this all becomes.

Remember those templates we talked about? They're training wheels, not a crutch. As you get more comfortable, start improvising. Develop your own style. Eventually, you want to get to a point where you can craft a killer message on the fly, tailored to each unique situation.

But don't just focus on your texting game. Work on yourself as a whole. Hit the gym, develop some interesting hobbies, and read a book once in a while. The more you have going on in your life, the more you'll have to talk about, and the more attractive you'll be. It's not rocket science, people.

Now, I know what you're thinking. "But isn't this all about getting laid?" Well, yes and no.

Sure, if you apply what you've learned here, you're probably going to see an uptick in your success rate. But if that's all you're focused on, you're missing the bigger picture. It's about more than just getting laid. It's about becoming the best version of yourself. It's about gaining confidence, not just in your dating life, but in every aspect of your existence. As you start to see success in your interactions with women, you'll notice something weird happening. You'll start feeling more confident in other areas of your life too. Suddenly, you're speaking up more at work. You're trying new things. You're taking risks you never would have before. That's the real magic here. We're not just teaching you how to text women. We're teaching you how to connect with people, how to present yourself in the best possible light, and how to be interesting and engaging. These are skills that will serve you well in every facet of your life.

So enjoy this quest. Embrace the awkward moments, the rejections, the fuck-ups. They're all part of the process.

And here's a little secret: women can smell desperation from a mile away. But you know what they find irresistible? A man who's comfortable in his own skin. A man who's constantly working on himself, not for others, but for his own satisfaction. That's the kind of confidence that's more attractive than any pickup line or clever text. So yes, use what you've learned here to improve your dating life. But don't stop there. Use it as a springboard to improve your whole damn life. At the end of the day, the most important relationship you'll ever have is the one with yourself.

What separates the men from the boys in this game? The ability to take feedback without turning into a whiny little puppy. That's right, I'm talking about the dreaded R-word: Reviews. Now, I know the thought of someone critiquing your performance might make your balls shrivel up faster than a polar bear's nutsack in the Arctic, but take a deep breath. Feedback is like a bloody goldmine of information. But you need to be man enough to ask for it. So here's what you're going to do. After you've put this book's teachings into practice, after you've had some successes (and inevitably, some epic failures), I want you to man up and ask for a review. And I'm not talking about asking your mom or your best friend who's been in the friendzone since high school. I'm talking about asking the women you've interacted with.

"But won't that be awkward as heck?" you ask. You're damn right it will be. But you know what's more awkward? Continuing to suck at dating because you're too chicken shit to find out what you're doing wrong.

Here's how you do it: After a date or a particularly good conversation, simply ask, "Hey, I'm always looking to improve. Is there anything I could have done better?" Boom. Simple as that. No need to make it weird or turn it into a therapy session. Just a straightforward question. Now, here's the hard part: you need to listen to what they say without getting defensive. If they say your jokes fell flatter than a pancake, don't argue. If they say your attempt at flirting was drier than the Sahara, don't try to justify yourself. Just shut up, listen, and take mental notes.

Just, don't just ask the women who seem into you!

The ones who ghosted you? The ones who turned you down? They're a fucking goldmine of information. If you can swallow your pride and ask them for feedback, you'll learn more than you ever would from a hundred successes. Sure, rejection stings. Criticism can feel like a kick in the nuts. But you know what's worse? Never improving because you're too scared to hear the truth. So sack up, buttercup. The road to dating success is paved with bruised egos and constructive criticism.

Your Gateway to Dating Nirvana

You've made it this far. You've absorbed more knowledge about dating and self-improvement than you probably thought possible. But my friend, we're just getting started.

See that QR code? That's not just some fancy decoration. That's your all-access pass to the holy grail of hookups. Scan that bad boy!

Also, provide your feedback on the book. We read every single review. The good, the bad, and the ugly. We take it all in and use it to make our stuff even better. If this book helped you, let us know. If it didn't, tell us why. Your feedback isn't just stroking our egos. It's helping us create better resources to help more gents. And who knows? If your feedback is particularly insightful (or hilariously bad), it might even make it into the next edition. Imagine that, your dating failures are immortalized in print. Your mom would be so proud!

The Final Countdown:
Get Off Your Ass and Do Something

Reading this book doesn't magically transform you into a dating guru any more than reading a book about fitness gives you six-pack abs. You need to get off your ass and do the work.

So here's your homework:

1. Take one piece of advice from this book and apply it today. Right freaking now.
2. Set a goal for yourself. Maybe it's getting five new matches this week. Maybe it's finally asking out that barista you've been eyeing for months. Whatever it is, write it down and make it happen.
3. Scan that QR code and dive into the additional resources. Your education isn't over, it's just beginning.
4. Leave an honest review. Good, bad, or ugly, we want to hear it all.
5. And most importantly, keep pushing yourself. Keep improving. Keep embracing the journey.

Becoming a master of dating is about continuous improvement, learning from your mistakes, and never settling for mediocrity.

You've got the tools. You've got the knowledge. Now it's time to get out there. And hey, if you end up in a happy relationship because of this book, you better bloody invite me to the wedding.

REFERENCES

A comprehensive guide to capturing the perfect profile picture. (2023, April 22). Gavin Jowitt. *https://www.gavinjowitt.com/blog/a-comprehensive-guide-to-capturing-the-perfect-profile-picture/*

Ackerman, C. (2024, March 14). What is self-confidence? + 9 Proven ways to increase it. PositivePsychology. *https://positivepsychology.com/self-confidence/*

Ackerman, C. E. (2018, July 5). Positive mindset: How to develop a positive mental attitude. PositivePsychology. *https://positivepsychology.com/positive-mindset/*

Attraction. (n.d.). Spark Notes. *https://www.sparknotes.com/psychology/psych101/socialpsychology/section6/*

Barnes, M. (2023, December 20). 300+ Deep questions to keep the conversation going. Science of People. *https://www.scienceofpeople.com/keep-conversation-going/*

Barton, J. J. S., & Corrow, S. L. (2016). Recognizing and identifying people: A neuropsychological review. Cortex, 75(10.1016/j.cortex.2015.11.023), 132–150. *https://doi.org/10.1016/j.cortex.2015.11.023*

BetterHelp Editorial Team. (2024, April 22). Understanding the science of attraction. BetterHelp. *https://www.betterhelp.com/advice/attachment/how-does-the-science-of-attraction-work/*

Bien, H. (2024, February 16). 17 Expert-approved first date tips to leave a lasting impression. The Knot. *https://www.theknot.com/content/first-date-tips*

Black, S. C. (2017). To cross or not to cross: Ethical boundaries in psychological practice. JANZSSA - Journal of the Australian and New Zealand Student Services Association, 25(1), 1339. *https://janzssa.scholasticahq.com/article/1339-to-cross-or-not-to-cross-ethical-boundaries-in-psychological-practice*

Bobby, L. M. (2023, July 17). Reacting vs. responding: Communication 101. Growing Self Counseling & Coaching. *https://www.growingself.com/reacting-versus-responding/*

Body Mind and Soul Leave a Comment. (2024, April 7). These are the problems of modern dating. The Good Men Project. *https://goodmenproject.com/featured-content/these-are-the-problems-of-modern-dating/*

Bounce back from ghosting: A dating coach's action plan for men. (n.d.). IAIN MYLES. Retrieved July 29, 2024, from *https://www.iainmyles.com/blog/bounce-back-from-ghosting-men-dating-guide*

Buontempo, F. (2023, September 28). "It becomes frustrating for both people": Guys are sharing the common challenges they face in the dating world, and it's safe to say that dating in 2023 is rough. BuzzFeed. *https://www.buzzfeed.com/fabianabuontempo/dating-challenges-for-men*

Byrne, D. (1961). Interpersonal attraction and attitude similarity. American Psychological Association. *https://psycnet.apa.org/record/1962-06365-001*

Carefoot, H. (2023, August 15). 13 Top tips for nailing the perfect dating profile, according to dating and relationship experts. Well+Good. *https://www.wellandgood.com/how-to-write-dating-profile/*

Centeno, A. (2024, June 17). 7 Ways to build sexual tension with women through text. Real Men Real Style. *https://www.realmenrealstyle.com/build-sexual-tension/*

Cherry, K. (2023, March 15). First impressions: Everything you need to make a good first introduction. Verywell Mind. *https://www.verywellmind.com/make-a-good-first-impression-7197993*

Chesky, N. (2023, September 30). Incorporating humor in SMS: When and how to do it right. TextAI. *https://www.usetextai.com/blog/incorporating-humor-in-sms%3A-when-and-how-to-do-it-right*

christopher@avochato.com. (2019, September 20). Text message templates: What they are and why you should use them. Avochato. *https://blog.avochato.com/index.php/2019/08/20/text-message-templates-what-they-are-and-why-you-should-use-them*

Cook, B. (2021, June 2). Post-date communication dos & don'ts. The Daily Dot. *https://www.dailydot.com/via/post-date-dos-and-donts/*

Crafting narratives: Honing the art of storytelling. (n.d.). History through Fiction. Retrieved July 27, 2024, from *https://www.historythroughfiction.com/blog/crafting-narratives*

Daffin, L., & Lane, C. (n.d.). Module 12: Attraction. Pressbooks. *https://opentext.wsu.edu/social-psychology/chapter/module-12-attraction/*

Deering, S. (2023, December 13). A Therapist's top 7 strategies for stopping negative self-talk. Real Simple. *https://www.realsimple.com/how-to-stop-negative-self-talk-8385831*

Downey, G., & Feldman, S. I. (1996). Implications of rejection sensitivity for intimate relationships. Journal of Personality and Social Psychology, 70(6), 1327–1343. *https://doi.org/10.1037//0022-3514.70.6.1327*

Eharmony Editorial Team. (2023, November 22). First date tips to get you that second date. Eharmony. *https://www.eharmony.com/dating-advice/getting-to-know/first-date-tips/*

Escalate interaction. (n.d.). MicroFocus. Retrieved July 29, 2024, from https://docs.microfocus.com/SM/9.60/Hybrid/Content/BestPracticesGuide_PD/SeviceDeskBestPractice_streamlined/Escalate_Interaction_wizard.html

Finkelstein, D. (n.d.). The psychology of accountability: Motivation and responsibility. Tick Those Boxes. *https://tickthoseboxes.com.au/the-psychology-of-accountability-motivation-and-responsibility/*

and-responsibility/

First impressions. (n.d.). Psychology Today. *https://www.psychologytoday.com/us/basics/first-impressions*

Foulkes, L. (2021, April 28). How to have more meaningful conversations. Psyche. *https://psyche.co/guides/how-to-have-more-meaningful-conversations*

Garsha. (2023, October 20). Part 2: The art of attraction — Psychological hacks to boost your appeal. Medium. *https://medium.com/@garsha/part-2-the-art-of-attraction-psychological-hacks-to-boost-your-appeal-ee1e91355c54*

Geralyn Dexter. (2023, June 15). Signs of manipulative behavior. Verywell Health. *https://www.verywellhealth.com/manipulative-behavior-5214329#:~:text=Manipulative%20behavior%20occurs%20when%20a*

Gerk, R. (2020, October 28). Listening to your body's signals can prevent heartbreak. An Idea (by Ingenious Piece). *https://medium.com/an-idea/listening-to-your-bodys-signals-can-prevent-heartbreak-7120f85c6649*

Ghosting. (n.d.). Psychology Today. *https://www.psychologytoday.com/us/basics/ghosting#:~:text=Ghosting%20is%20abruptly%20ending%20communication*

Gregory French. (2023, April 14). Storytelling is all about connecting to others. Atlas Accessories. *https://atlasaccessories.com/blogs/blog/storytelling-is-all-about-connecting-to-others*

Grey, L. (2018, February 6). Create an online dating profile that gets results. Medium; Medium. *https://medium.com/@laura_81682/create-an-online-dating-profile-that-gets-results-e38380be1aac*

Gupta, S. (2023, June 28). 50 Deep conversation starters for meaningful connections. Verywell Mind. *https://www.verywellmind.com/deep-conversation-starters-7548671*

Hailey, L. (2024a, April 29). What to text after the first date (show them you're serious). Science of People. *https://www.scienceofpeople.com/text-after-first-date/*

Hailey, L. (2024b, June 15). Be an expert at witty banter...How to charm with your words. Science of People. *https://www.scienceofpeople.com/witty-banter/*

Influence & integrity the essence of leadership series: Integrity. (2023, November 4). Stand Tall Steve. *https://www.standtallsteve.com/blog/influence-integrity-the-essence-of-leadership-series-integrity*

Jasheway, L. A. (2016, January 26). How to write better using humor. Writer's Digest. *https://www.writersdigest.com/write-better-fiction/how-to-mix-humor-into-your-writing*

Jbara, I. (2023, January 31). How to turn flirty texting into a real date. WikiHow. *https://www.wikihow.com/Move-from-Texting-to-Dating*

Jelen, B. (2022, June 15). Convert text dates to real dates. Mrexcel.com. *https://www.mrexcel.com/excel-tips/convert-text-dates-to-real-dates/*

Jonason, P. K., Luevano, V. X., & Adams, H. M. (2012). How the Dark Triad traits predict relationship choices. Personality and Individual Differences, 53(3), 180–184. https://doi.org/10.1016/j.paid.2012.03.007

Jonason, P. K., & Webster, G. D. (2011, December 21). A protean approach to social influence: Dark Triad personalities and social influence tactics. ResearchGate; Elsevier. https://www.researchgate.net/publication/257045293_A_protean_approach_to_social_influence_Dark_Triad_personalities_and_social_influence_tactics

Khan, T. (n.d.). Custom templates: Why they matter & how to create them. Contentcamel. Retrieved July 29, 2024, from https://www.contentcamel.io/5-ways-to-create-marketing-templates/

Kotsos, T. (2010, November 9). How to learn from your negative experiences. Mind Your Reality. https://mind-your-reality.com/negative-experiences.html#:~:text=By%20finding%20the%20belief(s

Lam, R. (2024, January 30). The characteristics of universal attractiveness. Medium. https://medium.com/@13032765d/the-characteristics-of-universal-attractiveness-ed569232560b

Lebowicz, S. (2020, October 27). 19 Science-backed ways men can appear more attractive to women. The Independent. https://www.independent.co.uk/life-style/love-sex/19-scienc-men-can-appear-more-attractive-women-dating-romance-a7674331.html

Lencioni, A. (2018, November 21). The dating playbook: 16 Ways to bounce back from breakups and Rejection. ParkBench Psychotherapy. https://adamlencioni.com/the-dating-playbook-16-ways-to-bounce-back-from-break-ups-and-rejection/

Lickerman, A. (2010, June 14). The diffusion of responsibility. Psychology Today. https://www.psychologytoday.com/intl/blog/happiness-in-world/201006/the-diffusion-responsibility

Little, A. C., Jones, B. C., & DeBruine, L. M. (2011). Facial attractiveness: evolutionary based research. Philosophical Transactions of the Royal Society B: Biological Sciences, 366(1571), 1638–1659. https://doi.org/10.1098/rstb.2010.0404

Lovering, N. (2024, May 14). Understanding dark psychology and manipulation tactics. Psych Central. https://psychcentral.com/disorders/dark-psychology#:~:text=What%20is%20dark%20psychology%3F

M, B. (n.d.). Flirty banter examples: How to turn any playful banter into flirting. The Art of Charm. Retrieved July 29, 2024, from https://theartofcharm.com/art-of-dating/a-mindset-that-can-turn-any-playful-banter-into-flirting-with-examples/

Macharia, E. (2023, September 16). 8 Psychological attraction tricks women CAN'T resist! LinkedIn. https://www.linkedin.com/pulse/8-psychological-attraction-tricks-women-cant-resist-eric-macharia/

Marie, V. (2019, November 15). Rules to creating a winning dating profile that wows. Medium; Medium. https://medium.com/@venessamperry/rules-to-creating-a-winning-dating-profile-ffd221ad0246

McKay, B., & McKay, K. (2015, August 6). How to initiate contact with a woman via text: The dos and don'ts of crafting a charming and effective first message. The Art of Manliness. https://www.artofmanliness.com/people/relationships/how-to-text-message-a-woman/

Mind. (2022, March). Managing stress and building resilience. Mind. https://www.mind.org.uk/information-support/types-of-mental-health-problems/stress/managing-stress-and-building-resilience/

Mind Tools Content Team. (n.d.). SMART goals. Mind Tools; Mind Tools. https://www.mindtools.com/a4wo118/smart-goals

Monahan, J. B. (2018, October 4). Trusting your intuition. Medium. https://medium.com/@jennifermonahan_28426/trusting-your-intuition-4a662e9f68ee

Montoya, R. M., & Horton, R. S. (2012). A meta-analytic investigation of the processes underlying the similarity-attraction effect. Journal of Social and Personal Relationships, 30(1), 64–94. https://doi.org/10.1177/0265407512452989

Morin, A. (2023, December 6). Understanding rejection sensitivity and how it can affect you. Verywell Mind. https://www.verywellmind.com/what-is-rejection-sensitivity-4682502

Morin, A. (2024, April 29). How to be more confident: 9 Tips that work. Verywell Mind. https://www.verywellmind.com/how-to-boost-your-self-confidence-4163098

Mrkonjić, E. (2022, April 28). What is dark psychology? Key concepts explained. SeedScientific. https://seedscientific.com/psychology/what-is-dark-psychology/

Nomad, D. D. T. (2023, August 21). The evolution of online romance in 2023: Digital dating. Medium. *https://drdiplextechnomad.medium.com/the-evolution-of-online-romance-in-2023-digital-dating-4313e18cba67*

O'Connor, C. (2023, February 28). How to keep a conversation going: 20 Techniques that work. Yesware. *https://www.yesware.com/blog/how-to-keep-a-conversation-going/*

Pandey, S. (2023, September 4). Dark psychology 101: What it is and why you need to know about it. Reveal the dark secrets of the human mind. Medium; Medium. *https://medium.com/@waytocognition/dark-psychology-101-what-it-is-and-why-you-need-to-know-about-it-db44d809662e*

Patil, J. (2024, July 18). 210+ New icebreaker questions that aren't cheesy. Toggl Blog. *https://toggl.com/blog/icebreaker-questions*

Peyton Nguyen. (2023, December 10). Consent culture: What consent means and how to set your own boundaries. Boston University. *https://www.bu.edu/articles/2023/consent-culture-what-consent-means-and-how-to-set-personal-boundaries/*

Philipp-Muller, A., Wallace, L. E., Sawicki, V., Patton, K. M., & Wegener, D. T. (2020). Understanding when similarity-induced affective attraction predicts willingness to affiliate: An attitude strength perspective. Frontiers in Psychology, 11(10.3389/fpsyg.2020.01919). *https://doi.org/10.3389/fpsyg.2020.01919*

Pogosyan, M. (2024, March 22). Tell a story build a connection. Psychology Today. *https://www.psychologytoday.com/us/blog/between-cultures/202403/tell-a-story-to-build-a-connection*

Prasad, C. (2022, September 5). 12 Benefits of SMS templates. JookSMS. *https://www.jooksms.com/blog/12-benefits-of-sms-templates/*

Propinquity effect. (n.d.). Psychology Concepts. *https://psychologyconcepts.com/propinquity-effect/#:~:text=The%20propinquity%20effect%20is%20a*

Pryor, S. (n.d.). 50 Topics to spark good conversation. SignUpGenius. *https://www.signupgenius.com/groups/good-conversation-topics.cfm*

Reierson, K. (2023, June 18). The importance of confidence in effective communication. ILLUMINATION. *https://medium.com/illumination/the-importance-of-confidence-in-effective-communication-a1fb66e2a5d5*

Reilly, C. (2023, October 16). The before, during, and after of a great first date. Style Girlfriend. *https://stylegirlfriend.com/first-date-tips-for-men/*

Rhyana Ebanks-Babb. (2023, March 8). The ultimate guide to ghosting: Understanding what it is, the impact, and how to overcome it. Team TMH. *https://www.talkingmentalhealth.com/post/ultimate-guide-ghosting-impact-overcome*

Rosa-Aquino, P., & Harrington, R. (2023, January 17). 11 Qualities in men that women find attractive, according to science. Business Insider. *https://www.businessinsider.com/science-backed-qualities-in-men-women-like-2016-6*

Ross, A., & Palšytė, G. (2024, April 14). "It makes us feel like creeps": 25 Men share their issues with modern dating. Bored Panda. *https://www.boredpanda.com/men-modern-dating-problems/*

Rowh, M. (2012, November). First impressions count. American Psychological Association. *https://www.apa.org/gradpsych/2012/11/first-impressions*

Ruby. (2022, September 10). How to transition from texting to an actual date. Good Gentleman. *https://goodgentleman.com/how-to-transition-from-texting-to-an-actual-date/*

Ruby. (2023, May 11). Text to send after a first date. Good Gentleman. *https://goodgentleman.com/text-to-send-after-a-first-date/*

Scenario. (2023, March 27). The art of the perfect PFP: How to create a powerful and unique profile picture using Scenario by @infoKG. Medium. *https://blog.scenario.com/the-art-of-the-perfect-pfp-how-to-create-a-powerful-and-unique-profile-picture-using-scenario-by-1f3482889b23*

Schmid, K. L., Rivers, S. E., Latimer, A. E., & Salovey, P. (2008). Targeting or Tailoring? Maximizing Resources to Create Effective Health Communications. Marketing Health Services, 28(1), 32–37. *https://www.ncbi.nlm.nih.gov/pmc/articles/PMC2728473/*

Scott, E. (2023, November 22). The toxic effects of negative self-talk. Verywell Mind. *https://www.verywellmind.com/negative-self-talk-and-how-it-affects-us-4161304*

Sharabi, L. (n.d.). Dating in the digital age. Psychology Today. *https://www.psychologytoday.com/us/blog/dating-in-the-digital-age*

SMART goals: A how-to guide. (2017). University of California. *https://www.ucop.edu/local-human-resources/_files/performance-appraisal/How%20to%20write%20SMART%20Goals%20v2.pdf*

Smithyman, T. (2023, May 31). How to handle rejection. Psyche. *https://psyche.co/guides/how-to-handle-rejection-so-that-you-can-heal-and-move-on*

Stone, R. (2019, April 22). Boundaries and consent. Medium. *https://medium.com/@RookStone/boundaries-and-consent-95945291ed90*

Strategies to captivate and engage women. (n.d.). FasterCapital. Retrieved July 27, 2024, from *https://fastercapital.com/topics/strategies-to-captivate-and-engage-women.html*

The Marketing Hustle. (2023, November 29). Decision fatigue: The paradox of too much choice. Medium. *https://medium.com/@dplayer/decision-fatigue-the-paradox-of-too-much-choice-43a8b8a7919b*

The Power of Hope. (2023, May 2). The art and science of conversations. Psychology Today. *https://www.psychologytoday.com/us/articles/202305/the-art-and-science-of-great-conversations*

Tulsiani, R. (2024, April 6). The power of multimedia in eLearning: Maximizing engagement and retention. ELearning Industry. *https://elearningindustry.com/the-power-of-multimedia-in-learning-maximizing-engagement-and-retention#:~:text=Strategic%20Integration%20Of%20Multimedia%20In%20Learning&text=Avoid%20unnecessary%20or%20decorative%20additions*

225 Conversation starters for any situation. (n.d.). Gifts.com Blog. *https://www.gifts.com/blog/conversation-starters*

Vaia Editorial Team. (n.d.). Physical attractiveness. Vaia. Retrieved July 9, 2024, from *https://www.vaia.com/en-us/explanations/psychology/relationships/physical-attractiveness/*

Vogels, E., & Anderson, M. (2020, May 8). Dating and relationships in the digital age. Pew Research Center; Pew Research Center. *https://www.pewresearch.org/internet/2020/05/08/dating-and-relationships-in-the-digital-age/*

Vohs, K. D., Baumeister, R. F., Schmeichel, B. J., Twenge, J. M., Nelson, N. M., & Tice, D. M. (2008). Making choices impairs subsequent self-control: A limited-resource account of decision making, self-regulation, and active initiative. Journal of Personality and Social Psychology, 94(5), 883–898. *https://doi.org/10.1037/0022-3514.94.5.883*

Wei, M. (2024, May 31). 4 Ways to cultivate integrity for inner emotional balance. Center for Practical Wisdom | the University of Chicago. *https://wisdomcenter.uchicago.edu/news/wisdom-news/4-ways-cultivate-integrity-inner-emotional-balance*

Wells, J. (n.d.). 7 qualities women find most attractive in men. The Gentleman's Journal. *https://www.thegentlemansjournal.com/article/7-qualities-women-find-attractive-men/*

Wrench, J., Punyanunt-Carter, N., & Thweatt, K. (2020, August 19). 8.3: Stages of relationships. LibreTexts Social Sciences. *https://socialsci.libretexts.org/Bookshelves/Communication/Interpersonal_Communication/Interpersonal_Communication_-_A_Mindful_Approach_to_Relationships_(Wrench_et_al.)/08%3A_Building_and_Maintaining_Relationships/8.03%3A_Stages_of_Relationships*

Wu, K. (2017, February 14). Love, Actually: The science behind lust, attraction, and companionship. Science in the News; Harvard University. *https://sitn.hms.harvard.edu/flash/2017/love-actually-science-behind-lust-attraction-companionship/#:~:text=High%20levels%20of%20dopamine%20and*

Yildiz, M. (2023, November 17). What makes stories truly memorable and impactful and how to craft them. ILLUMINATION. *https://medium.com/illumination/what-makes-a-story-truly-memorable-and-impactful-and-why-b6b9afc768cf*

Young, K. (2016, February 12). 9 Ways to tap into your intuition (and why you'll want to). Hey Sigmund. *https://www.heysigmund.com/9-ways-to-tap-into-your-intuition-and-why-youll-want-to/*

Zhou, A. (2023, February 22). Effective communication: Tailoring the message to each audience. Tech Lead Hub. *https://medium.com/tech-lead-hub/effective-communication-tailoring-the-message-to-each-audience-31f1cbbc64cc*

Image References

Akyurt, E. (2019). Standing Man Figurine [Image]. In Pexels. *https://www.pexels.com/photo/standing-man-figurine-2098604/*

Ann H. (2021). A Love Emoticon on Blue Surface [Image]. In Pexels. *https://www.pexels.com/photo/a-love-emoticon-on-blue-surface-7313448/*

Ann H. (2022). Question and Answer Letters and an Exclamation and Question Marks [Image]. In Pexels. *https://www.pexels.com/photo/question-and-answer-letters-and-an-exclamation-and-question-marks-11183364/*

Augusts, A. (2020). Because I love Lego and I have a lot of these minifigures! [Image]. In Unsplash. *https://unsplash.com/photos/lego-mini-figure-on-red-chair-vhnljj9RkV8*

Cup of Couple. (2021). Hand Holding Blank Speech Bubble [Image]. In Pexels. *https://www.pexels.com/photo/hand-holding-blank-speech-bubble-8015676/*

Đàng Thiện Thanh Tài. (2020). Child in ghost costume sitting in park [Image]. In Pexels. *https://www.pexels.com/photo/child-in-ghost-costume-sitting-in-park-6331533/*

DESIGNECOLOGIST. (2018). Prick [Image]. In Unsplash. *https://unsplash.com/photos/assorted-cactus-decors-on-file-cabinet-6kIhClasj3Q*

Diana. (2018). [Image]. In Pexels. *https://www.pexels.com/photo/black-and-white-vhs-tape-on-white-wooden-surface-1302308/*

Eliason, K. (2019). Man in bunny costume in mid air in time lapse photography [Image]. In Unsplash. *https://unsplash.com/photos/man-in-bunny-costume-in-mid-air-in-time-lapse-photography-IF8B82QBCkM*

Girl with red hat. (2021). Clear blue array of nokia's 6110 on white background. [Image]. In Unsplash. *https://unsplash.com/photos/black-and-silver-candybar-phone-ma2ur_ld0ko*

Jess Bailey Designs. (2017). Black Pencil Screenshot [Image]. In Pexels. *https://www.pexels.com/photo/black-pencil-screenshot-750913/*

Leonov, A. (2019). Albert Einstein [Image]. In Unsplash. *https://unsplash.com/photos/a-person-holding-up-a-yellow-face-mask-P5nZwlbTngI*

Lopez, A. (2018). [Image]. In Unsplash. *https://unsplash.com/photos/brown-wooden-dresser-with-mirror-inside-white-room-JR1ChBgzJvQ*

Monstera Production. (2020). Cutout paper composition of yellow signboard with exclamation mark [Image]. In Pexels. *https://www.pexels.com/photo/cutout-paper-composition-of-yellow-signboard-with-exclamation-mark-5849597/*

Pădureț, D. C. (2020). [Image]. In Unsplash. *https://unsplash.com/photos/silver-and-gold-round-coins-BxgVEo_rF-o*

Piacquadio, A. (2020). Portrait Photo of a Skeleton in Sunglasses and Wig [Image]. In Pexels. *https://www.pexels.com/photo/portrait-photo-of-a-skeleton-in-sunglasses-and-wig-3756616/*

SHRESTHA, B. K. (2022). [Image]. In Unsplash. *https://unsplash.com/photos/a-close-up-of-a-human-brain-on-a-white-background-iW_n3MqVVtU*

Sincerely Media. (2021). [Image]. In Unsplash. *https://unsplash.com/photos/logo-JpwqcZwZcMo*

Winkler, M. (2020). Emoji Backgrounds [Image]. In Unsplash. *https://unsplash.com/photos/black-flat-screen-tv-turned-on-displaying-yellow-emoji-wpOa2i3MUrY*

愚木混株 cdd20. (2022). [Image]. In Unsplash. *https://unsplash.com/photos/a-black-background-with-a-red-and-yellow-dotted-arrow-gm6g-22Nzro*

Made in the USA
Las Vegas, NV
05 December 2024

6125bcba-d605-4cc4-b0b5-021243ebd813R01